NASCAR NOW!

NASCAR NOW!

THIRD EDITION
TIMOTHY MILLER
& STEVE MILTON

FIREFLY BOOKS

A Firefly Book

Published by Firefly Books Ltd. 2008

First printing

Publisher Cataloging-in-Publication Data (U.S.)
Miller, Timothy, 1951-
    NASCAR now! / by Timothy Miller ; and Steve Milton.
    3rd ed.
[ ] p. : col. photos. ; cm.
Includes index.
Summary: Guide to NASCAR, and auto and stock car racing, including their history, biographies of drivers, analysis of racing teams, and NASCAR primer, rules and conduct.
ISBN-13: 978-1-55407-340-5 (pbk.)
ISBN-10: 1-55407-340-5 (pbk.)
1. NASCAR (Association). 2. Stock car racing – United States. 3. Automobile racing drivers – United States. I. Milton, Steve.   II. Title.
796.72/0973 dc22   GV1029.9 S74M56 2008

Library and Archives Canada Cataloguing in Publication
Miller, Timothy, 1951-
    NASCAR now! / Timothy Miller and Steve Milton. – 3rd ed.
ISBN-13: 978-1-55407-340-5 (pbk.)
ISBN-10: 1-55407-340-5 (pbk.)
1. NASCAR (Association). 2. Stock car racing – United States. 3. Automobile racing drivers – United States. I. Milton, Steve II. Title.
GV1029.9.S74M54
2008   796.720973   C2008-901125-2

Published in the United States by
Firefly Books (U.S.) Inc.
P.O. Box 1338, Ellicott Station
Buffalo, New York 14205

Published in Canada by
Firefly Books Ltd.
66 Leek Crescent
Richmond Hill, Ontario L4B 1H1

Cover and interior design by Gareth Lind / LINDdesign

Printed in China

The publisher gratefully acknowledges the financial support for our publishing program by the Government of Canada through the Book Publishing Industry Development Program.

NASCAR NOW! is dedicated to all the fans in the NASCAR world. You have made the sport what it is today.

Photo Credits

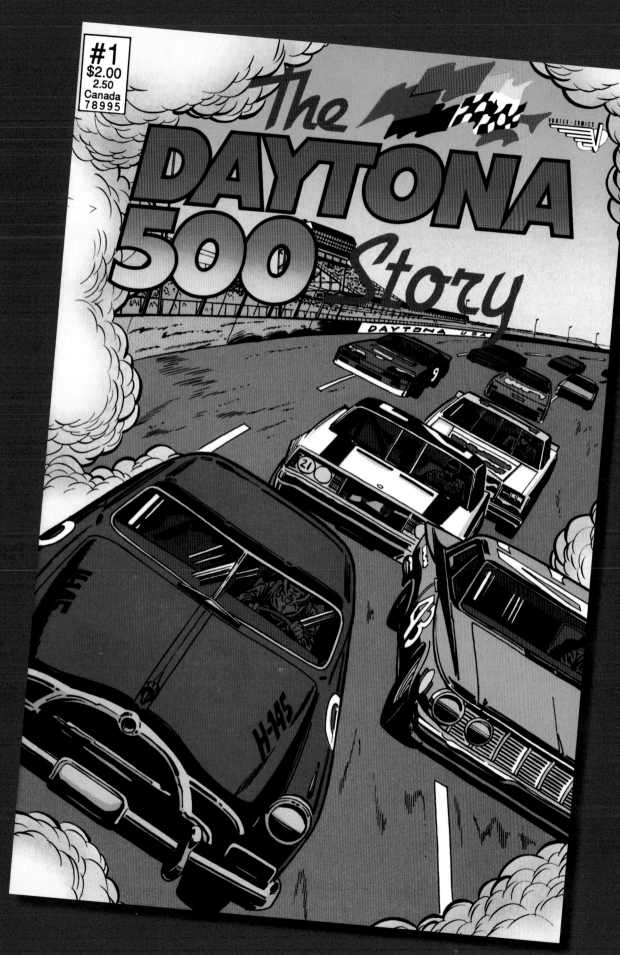

Published by Vortex Comics in 1991, *The Daytona 500 Story* offered a colorful and informative history of the race.

Previous page: Jimmie Johnson (48) and Michael Waltrip (55) pace the field for the 50th running of the Daytona 500, billed by NASCAR as "America's Great Race."

CONTENTS

START YOUR ENGINES

NASCAR is a sport. NASCAR is entertainment. NASCAR is a cultural and economic phenomenon.

From a modest start centered mainly in the southern U.S. states, NASCAR stock car racing has exploded to the forefront of the sporting and cultural world in the past decade. It has surpassed older traditional sports in attendance, media attention and merchandise marketing. Also, through strong business acumen, NASCAR has become a financial giant.

NASCAR has come a long way from the races on the beaches in Florida and the dusty dirt tracks south of the Mason-Dixon Line. Through planning, insightful growth, and solid marketing and promotion, NASCAR has succeeded beyond all expectations.

NASCAR's popularity stems from its relatively simple racing machines that resemble the cars seen in everyday life that fans can relate to. And the stars of NASCAR, the drivers, are approachable athletes from humble beginnings who are quite willing to put back into the sport what they reap from it.

For 36 weekends a year, hundreds of thousands of fans, and millions more via television, witness the color, the noise and the excitement as dozens of sleek race cars and compelling drivers provide heart-stopping action in a competition like no other.

More than six million people attend

NASCAR Sprint Cup races annually, with an estimated 275 million watching the races on national broadcasts across the globe. Billions of dollars are invested in sponsorship and promotion, and licensed NASCAR merchandise tops $2 billion per year. Each of the 36 Sprint Cup events averages 186,000 spectators. One Cup race draws more fans than the Super Bowl, a World Series Baseball game, and an NBA finals game combined.

Cup drivers are revered as folk heroes, and some have become idols on a national scale as part of the fabric of society. Driver rivalries are intense, as is the competition among auto manufacturers.

When compared to other major league sports, NASCAR races have unique presentations. Each race stands on its own as a major event with its own sense of urgency and importance, not unlike a playoff game in another sport. There is only one Cup race a week, so there's only one opportunity to view the race, and a concentrated effort is made to get the most from each weekly event.

NASCAR's stock car racing has grown to unprecedented levels not only as a major sport but as a part of our daily lives. The racing entity that Bill France envisioned in 1949 has grown over the past five decades, and to this day the tradition is upheld by the France family as it takes NASCAR to the next stage of sports entertainment.

NASCAR NOW! *ushers in a new era in NASCAR racing.*

After years of development, the Car of Tomorrow has become reality. The CoT functions like a salary cap in other major sports, leveling the playing field by allowing only a fixed amount of money to be spent for competition. In this new edition, you'll catch up on the story of the CoT's development and details of the thinking behind the new car style.

The four manufacturers all have new car models in competition, including Chevrolet's iconic Impala name, which, in CoT trim, won its first victory since 1963 in the first CoT race in March of 2007.

Another major development in NASCAR Sprint Cup racing has been the influx of former open-wheel race car drivers to the world of full-fendered stock car racing.

Colombian Juan Pablo Montoya, a former CART Champ Car champion, a former Formula One driver, and a former 24 Hours of Daytona winner, has successfully made the transition to stock cars. He placed 20th in the 2007 standings in his rookie year.

And open-wheel aces such as Patrick Carpentier, Dario Franchitti and Sam Hornish Jr. are now all climbing into their stock cars.

NASCAR NOW! covers the entire scope of this engrossing sport, from its beginnings to its present action-packed season. Along with a history of the sport, you'll learn about some of the colorful personalities that helped make NASCAR what it is today. You'll follow the evolution of the NASCAR stock car, including the newest safety technology, and find out more about the tracks and how the drivers win points, as well as the marketing machine that has fueled the sport. You'll experience the drama of pit stops and meet the hottest and most influential drivers of the present NASCAR scene.

You'll also read about some of NASCAR's early ventures aside from stock car racing. And you'll get the latest about the new NASCAR Hall of Fame in Charlotte.

So get buckled up and press that starter. It's time for the green flag.

Opposite: Cup rookie Michael McDowell fires up his Aaron's Dream Machine Toyota at the start of the Goody's Cool Orange 500. He started 34th and finished 26th.

The start of the first NASCAR Strictly Stock race, in June of 1949, on the dirt oval of the New Charlotte Speedway in Charlotte, NC. There are Fords, Oldsmobiles, Hudsons, Buicks, and even a Lincoln in the photo. Note the absence of any sponsors on the cars, and the whitewall tires on the Ford in the front.

The real roots of stock car racing go back more than 100 years to the introduction of the automobile.

Motoring contests were held in Europe and North America during the auto's formative years, but the contests were quite different in makeup on each side of the Atlantic Ocean.

European and British racing was performed in rallies on local roads and thoroughfares. Spectators lined streets and country roads as cars roared past them only feet away. Eventually this road racing was curtailed with the advent of specially designed and constructed circuits that continue to this day.

In North America, road racing was the mainstay of early competition, but automobiles were expensive and the drivers were usually wealthy sportsmen. By 1910, with the arrival of Ford's Model T, automobiles were more afford-able for the ordinary person, and anyone with a competitive spirit and strong arms could go racing.

But where to race? Aside from populated areas in the eastern United States, most roads were nothing more than wagon paths, and extensive auto travel was virtually impossible. So races were held at county fairgrounds, where there were already smooth oval-shaped horse-racing tracks.

By World War I, racing on these dirt ovals had become very popular. Carl Fisher's 2.5-mile brick-paved oval just outside of

Indianapolis, built in 1909, took racing to new levels. A multitude of wooden-surfaced board tracks, successors to bicycle velodromes, surfaced across the country in the next 20 years.

While the Indy-style roadster developed through the 1930s, benefiting from the national sanction of the Contest Board of the American Automobile Association, smaller versions of these cars, such as Sprint and Midget cars, plied the local fairgrounds, especially in the northeast and midwest states.

A movement was also taking place in the southern states, some of which has been romanticized to the point that it's now hard to tell fact from fiction. But it did have an influence in the history of stock car racing.

In their efforts to outrun government agents with cars full of illegally made whiskey, "moonshine" runners were modifying stock street cars and becoming quite successful at delivering the goods. The car of choice was usually the light, nimble and fast V8-powered Ford.

Soon the "shine" runners, along with car owners with regular jobs, wanted to pit their driving talents against each other, so informal contests started, usually on a hastily built dirt oval in a farm field. As these impromptu contests grew and became popular, family and friends would appear to compete for the bragging rights. Bleachers were built, hot dogs sold and prize money awarded.

To the north, full-fendered "stock" car racing, known as "jalopy" or "modified" racing, was a mainstay on the ovals along with the AAA Indy-type cars. But these "stock" cars were far from stock, with their modified engines, suspensions, and cut-down bodywork. The cars of the south were more stock-like in appearance.

But there was no unity among all the racers and tracks. Each track had its own set of rules and car specs. There was no overall governing body such as the AAA's Contest Board.

Enter Bill France. An auto mechanic from the Washington D.C. area, France moved to Daytona Beach on Florida's east coast in 1934 and set up shop. He continued to race his

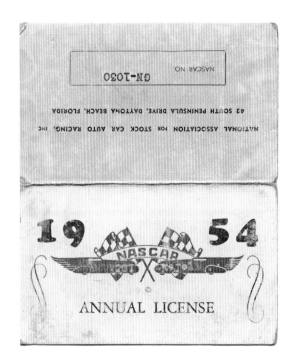

An early annual competitor license, issued six years after NASCAR was officially incorporated. This holder of this card was a race driver from Canada.

Modified in Florida and successfully promoted some small beach/road events at Daytona, but by the end of World War II he was thinking about a national sanctioning body that could oversee this type of racing. The AAA wasn't interested in racing cars that looked like anything you could drive off a car lot.

After meetings with other promoters, car owners and drivers just before Christmas of 1947, the foundations were laid, and in February, 1948, the National Association for Stock Car Auto Racing was legally incorporated.

For the first two years of its existence, NASCAR ran only a Modified class, but France believed if fans could identify with the cars on the tracks, they would bond with the sport. France's vision and hard work took life in 1949 with NASCAR's new Strictly Stock division. Organized stock car racing was born.

The first race in this class was held in June,1949, at the new three-quarter mile Charlotte, NC, dirt track (now the Charlotte Speedway). With a purse of $2,000 and 13,000 fans to witness the event, the first NASCAR stock car race was won by Jim Roper in a Lincoln.

In the early 1950s NASCAR expanded from its Southern roots to travel west to California and Arizona, and north to Michigan. The showroom stock cars became less and less showroom in appearance and performance, sporting the largest engines available, more safety equipment, and heavy-duty brakes and suspensions.

As the decade progressed, more race tracks were built — substantial facilities with seating and amenities approaching baseball parks. As

Daytona Beach in 1957, the second last race at the Beach. A large crowd in the Florida sunshine is waiting for the race to begin. Lots of people, no stands, and no protection from a car careening into the crowd.

the sport grew, the new tracks were all paved.

Stock car racing reached a new level of maturity with the opening of the Daytona International Speedway in 1959. The brain-child of France, this 2.5-mile long oval with 31-degree corner banking was constructed on 480 acres of northern Florida land. The track was built to replace the 4.1-mile beach/road course oval that NASCAR ran on the Atlantic shore in February.

Cotton Owens set the pace in his Pontiac, with a top qualifying speed of over 143 mph for the first race. And in a dramatic photo-finish that decided the inaugural Daytona 500 race victor some days later, Lee Petty, in an Oldsmobile, was declared the winner over

John Beauchamp and his Thunderbird, who originally took the checkered flag.

Starting in the early 1960s, as some of its events were televized, NASCAR acquired many new fans. The sport grew in popularity and professionalism, and with the involvement of corporate sponsorship it became big business.

A new generation of drivers emerged. Car manufacturers built cars specifically to win races, and tire companies devoted personnel exclusively to race-car research and development. While this expansion was taking place, France ran NASCAR with a firm hand.

Richard Petty was the driver who brought NASCAR to prominence at this time. This lanky second-generation driver from North Carolina started his career in 1958 and remained the undisputed "King" of stock car racing until his retirement in 1992. Many of his accomplishments, such as his 200 career wins, may never be equaled. An immensely popular driver, Petty, with his series of Plymouths, became the sport's top ambassador. He spent almost as much time signing autographs for his fans at the track as he did behind the wheel, and he always gave back to the sport whatever he accomplished over his 35 years of racing.

In addition to NASCAR, another racing body was also involved in stock car racing during this era. When the AAA (American Automobile Association) dropped its involvement with auto racing in 1955, the United States Auto Club (USAC) was formed, and it became the sanctioning body for most open-wheeled racing, including Sprint, Midget, and Champ (Indy) car events.

USAC also had a stock car series and was prominent in areas other than the southern states. Although the USAC stock car series did not race as often as NASCAR, it provided some fierce competition with a lot of "box office" drivers of the day, well-known drivers such as A.J. Foyt, Parnelli Jones and Mario Andretti, who raced Champ cars at tracks such as Pocono, Milwaukee and, of course, Indy. But by 1970 USAC dropped its stock division, and continued with its open-wheeled classes.

In 1971, NASCAR entered what is considered its "modern" era. Tobacco giant R.J. Reynolds gave its financial support to NASCAR's top division, a relationship that grew and prospered until 2003. The Winston Cup was born.

Also at this time, television started taking an active role in presenting Winston Cup races, starting with ABC's "Wide World of Sports" broadcasts. With this new exposure, large corporations such as Coca-Cola, Proctor & Gamble, and STP began to see the potential of being financially involved in racing.

In 1979 the Daytona 500 became the first race to be televized live in its entirety. An estimated 20 million viewers watched Petty win this race as late-race leaders Cale Yarborough and Bobby Allison collided on the last lap, got out of their cars and started fighting while Petty took the checkered flag. All of this late-race action and drama, on and off the track, unfolded in front of millions of viewers and gave NASCAR a tremendous boost in popularity.

In the early 1980s, as Detroit started producing smaller, more fuel-efficient automobiles, NASCAR followed suit, and race cars were "downsized" with wheelbases of 110 inches for the new sedans. Also at this time, new drivers were making their mark in Winston Cup competition. Among the most prominent were Dale Earnhardt, Darrell Waltrip, Dale Jarrett and Bill Elliott.

One of the most controversial changes in stock car racing at the NASCAR level took place in 1987. With the ever-increasing racing speeds, safety became an important issue, and NASCAR instituted "restrictor plates," a device between the race car engine's carburetor and intake manifold. These plates reduce the fuel/air mixture into the engine, cutting down engine power, and hence reducing car speed. Restrictor plates are mandatory on the larger super speedways such as Daytona and Talladega.

Other safety developments have been instituted in the past few years, including roof flaps to reduce the possibility of cars becoming airborne, pit road rules and reduced pit lane speeds, and crash-absorbing barrier walls.

NASCAR has also expanded its track horizons over the past several years, replacing older, smaller tracks with new facilities such the Texas Motor Speedway to hold the legions of fans. Two road-racing circuits are now part of the 36-race schedule.

And growth in NASCAR took a big step forward in 1994, when the first Cup race was held at the Indianapolis Motor Speedway, the first race ever to be run at Indy aside from the Indianapolis 500 Memorial Day classic held since 1911. Winning the inaugural Brickyard 500 was a young Jeff Gordon, who would go on to capture the 1995 Winston Cup title.

Drivers such as Gordon, Dale Earnardt Jr., Matt Kenseth and Tony Stewart exemplify NASCAR's current driving superstars. Other prominent names include Jimmie Johnson, Clint Bowyer, Carl Edwards and the Busch Brothers, Kurt and Kyle.

In 2003, after a 32-year relationship, Reynolds ended its title sponsorship with NASCAR, and the wireless technology company Nextel Communications became the Cup series title sponsor.

At the start of the 2008 season, there were two major changes in NASCAR. After a corporate merger between Nextel and Sprint, a leader in the data communications and cellular phone industry, NASCAR's top series has become known as the Sprint Cup.

The other major change was the introduction of NASCAR's "Car of Tomorrow" on a full-time competition level. To standardize car building and offer enhanced driver safety, NASCAR developed a mandatory new platform in stock car racing. After several years of research and development, the CoT will now be driven exclusively at all Cup races.

Here's a mid-1950s Dodge getting the flag for a run along the Daytona beach. The Beach Trials were a part of NASCAR's Speedweek in February of each year, where stock and modified automobiles were clocked in measured distances (usually a mile). By the late 1950s the cars were getting too fast to speed along the sandy shoreline and the event was discontinued.

Flights of Fancy – the NASCAR Experiments

Since its inception in the late 1940s, NASCAR has sanctioned several different types and series of auto racing. Today, along with its premier series, the Sprint Cup, and the Nationwide Series, it sanctions the Craftsman Truck Series and several regional series throughout North America.

In its early years, NASCAR tried several different competition venues as it matured. Initially NASCAR started with the "Strictly Stock" series, which developed into the Grand National, then the Winston, Nextel, and Sprint Cup. At the start there also was the Modified division, which continues to this day.

But the Speedway Division? Midgets? Compacts? And drag racing? Yes, NASCAR tried all of these as well as being involved in other automotive competitions. Here are some of the more unique motorsport activities NASCAR has been associated with.

Beach Trials

Speed contests have been held ever since the invention of the automobile, and the flat expanses of beach on Florida's east cost were used for the first North American speed trials.

Initially held at Ormond Beach, the trials were moved south to Daytona Beach, and by the time NASCAR was formed, the Beach Trials were a major part of the Daytona Speedweek held in February, along with the running of the Daytona races on the original beach/highway course.

Initially, the cars were street cars that were timed through a mile course after getting a two-mile head start to get up to speed. There was also a standing-start mile.

But by the mid-1950s, these "stock" cars began looking and performing more like the race cars on NASCAR's Grand National circuit, complete with factory backing, professional mechanics and race drivers.

After winning the GN title in 1955, team owner Carl Kiekhaefer showed up at the Beach with one of his unbeatable Chrysler 300 entries. Prepared to the highest degree, and with team driver and champ Tim Flock at the wheel, the big car ran at almost 140 mph.

Zora Arkus-Duntov, the driving force behind the development of the Chevrolet Corvette, showed up in 1956 with a highly modified Corvette, complete with streamlined fin, and won the modified sports car class at 147 mph. By comparison, a basic stock Corvette driven by road-racing ace John Fitch was clocked at 86.8 mph.

While the Beach Trials were an important and popular part of Speedweek, the cars got too fast for safe running on the hard-packed sand, and by the late 1950s these land speed record attempts headed west to the Utah salt flats of Bonneville.

Compacts

When the "Big Three" (Ford, GM and Chrysler) brought out their smaller, compact cars in 1960, NASCAR scheduled races for them as part of the Daytona-based Speedweek. For the next couple of years, Falcons, Corvairs, Valiants and some foreign cars competed in the Beach Trials, and ran races on Daytona's 3.8-mile road course as well as a 20-lap oval-track event.

The first Compact race on Daytona's infield road course was dominated by Chrysler's

Valiant, which took the top four spots. Grand National driver Marvin Panch led from flag to flag.

In the 20-lapper on the big oval, Panch came from a lap behind to win in his Valiant, as the top four cars were taken out in a wreck. His average speed was 122 mph with a factory-modified Slant Six engine. But with little interest from the teams and the fans, NASCAR dropped the Compacts to concentrate on its other divisions.

Midgets

One of NASCAR's early rivals was Midget racing, which was very popular in other parts of North America away from NASCAR's southern base.

These scaled-down Sprint Cars with small Offenhauser or outboard motors, or Ford's 60-horsepower Flathead V8 engines were peppered all over the country, and NASCAR tried sanctioning the class in its home territory. Fans, however, were not impressed with the little cars, preferring the usual fare of big stock cars with which they could identify. NASCAR took note and discontinued the Midgets.

The Speedway Division

Another experiment in NASCAR's early years was the Speedway Division. In November of 1951, NASCAR announced it would form this new class, which featured Indy-style roadsters with domestic V8 engines. The newer Oldsmobile and Cadillac overhead valve V8 engines were popular. The GMC six-cylinder truck engine, and the Ford and Mercury Flathead V8 engines were also a mainstay, as there was a great deal of available speed equipment for these powerplants.

The class debuted during the Daytona Speedweek in February of 1952. Driving Penny Mullis' Cadillac Special, Buck Baker bested the other 10 cars on the measured mile with a 140–41-mph pass. Future Grand National star Fireball Roberts was second in his Ford-powered roadster.

Led by Darlington Raceway, the Speedway cars were lined up for seven races in 1952 on dirt tracks including Martinsville, Virginia, Rochester, New York, Atlanta, Georgia and the season-closer on the famous Langhorne, Pennsylvania, mile track.

But slim fields of cars plagued the division right from the start. When only 21 Speedway

Richard Petty, along with other Chrysler teams, sat out some of the 1965 NASCAR season to protest the banning of the powerful Hemi engine, which had been dominating the circuit. Instead of racing stock, Petty drag raced a home-built Barracuda nicknamed "Outlawed," and numbered "43 Jr." NASCAR and Chrysler soon made up, and Petty resumed his oval track career the next season.

cars showed up at Darlington rather than the expected 40, NASCAR's Bill France and Darlington's Harold Brasington added a 100-mile GN race to guarantee a profit-making crowd, as Darlington had put up a $10,000 purse for the 200-mile Speedway race.

Only 17 cars raced at Martinsville, and only seven cars were running when Tex Keene of

Curtis Turner and his Ford convertible at Daytona Beach in 1956. The soft-top division ran for several years, complimenting the Grand National division.

Georgia won the 100-miler. Even fewer cars — 14 — showed for the third event, a 100-miler at Rochester in May of 1952.

By June, 19 cars were on hand at Heidelberg, Pennsylvania, and 22 cars competed at Langhorne, but other events were cancelled. Buck Baker, who won the Darlington opener and finished several times in the top five, was declared the champion.

NASCAR tried again in 1953, but only eight cars were at Daytona. For the scheduled races, France merged the Speedway cars with the Sportsman class in the events, and the prize money dropped to $2,500, half of the year before. Only three races were run in 1953, all in North Carolina, and all with 11 cars or less.

As with the Midgets, fans in NASCAR's home territory weren't interested in the open-wheel racing of the Speedway Division. Fans couldn't relate the same way to the Midgets and Speedway cars as they could to the stock cars, cars they saw not only at the track but also on the street every day. Speedway cars were more expensive to build and race, keeping the car counts low.

Another aspect was sponsorship. It was a lot easier for a stock car driver or team to successfully lobby an auto dealership for support when the cars looked like everyday cars. The "win on Sunday, sell on Monday" axiom was a big part of racing sponsorship.

The Convertible Division

One racing division that NASCAR tried with success was its Convertible Division, started in 1956.

The cars were the same as the Grand National cars but had more substantial rollover protection. They also ran under the same rules as GN cars, and were highly popular with the fans, because they could watch their heroes "working in the office" as they sawed away on the large stock steering wheels of the day.

Curtis Turner was king of the division. He took 30 poles and 38 wins in his series of Ford ragtops from 1956 to 1959. He won 22 races in 1956 alone. Richard Petty won his first NASCAR race driving a 1957 Oldsmobile in 1959 at Columbia.

The Convertibles would usually be part of a double bill on a two-day NASCAR weekend. The Convertibles and the Modifieds would run together on Saturday, and the headlining GN cars on Sunday, not unlike what happens on a NASCAR race weekend of today, with three divisions over the same weekend at the same race facility.

But after a couple of seasons, the basic racer instinct of winning got the best of the division. As the rules between the GN cars and the Convertibles were essentially the same, racers took a Convertible and fashioned a roof for it so they could run in both classes with one car. But then the racers did the opposite, and used the GN-based sedan, with its roof removed, for the Convertible class. A comparable sedan, whether Ford, Chevy, Olds, or T-Bird, was much lighter than the soft-top.

After 1959, these zipper-top cars resembled neither sedan nor convertible, and the class was dropped, although Darlington ran a special Rebel 300 for the cars until 1962.

Drag Racing

NASCAR really got away from its traditional oval track ventures with a solid attempt at sanctioning drag racing.

There was some straight-line action as early as 1956 as part of the Daytona Beach Speedweek, but a major event was held four years later.

NHRA president Wally Parks and NHRA division director Ernie Schorb met with NASCAR vice-president Ed Otto and presented the week-long Winter Nationals at Daytona Beach's Spruce Creek Drag Strip in February of 1960. Florida racer and now legendary drag racing icon Don Garlits won enough races during the week to take the Top Eliminator award.

It wasn't until 1965 that drag racing returned to NASCAR and for the next two years, up to 29 strips operated under NASCAR, closely following NHRA rules and car classifications. Ed Witzberger headed up this division from his Pittsburgh, Pennsylvania, base. Most tracks were in Ohio, New Jersey, and Virginia, although there were some sanctions farther away, such as Niagara International in Western New York and the Cayuga dragstrip in Southern Ontario.

NASCAR highlighted its early drag racing with match races between some of its Grand National personalities. Fireball Roberts, Fred Lorenzen and Wendell Scott were among GN drivers that did some match racing. Richard Petty campaigned a Barracuda, and Cotton Owens built a crowd-pleasing rear-engined Dodge Dart station wagon called the Cotton Picker.

The 1966 program was highlighted with four national events, and there was a weekly tour package including races with Top Fuel dragster and Grand Stock. The shows had NASCAR's organizational expertise, good crowds, and good car counts. But by the end of 1967, NASCAR pulled the plug on drag racing. With lower car counts, and the NHRA moving into the east with an established and proven product, NASCAR returned to focus on what it did best in the racing world.

Top: All drag races, including NASCAR-sanctioned events, were started with a brave soul standing between the two cars as they took off. The starter was eventually replaced in the early 1960s, with the advent of the "Christmas Tree" electronic starting and timing system.

Bottom: An official classification guide for NASCAR-sanctioned drag strips from 1966. It listed all makes and models of domestic cars, along with engine sizes, giving the racers and track officials the information needed to pair up cars correctly in the various classes.

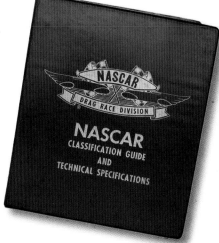

NASCAR 101

STOCK CARS

When NASCAR began its "Strictly Stock" division in 1949, the cars used in the racing were exactly that – stock. A racer could literally go to an auto dealership, buy a car off the lot, and go stock car racing. While the early drivers tried all types of coupes and sedans, the earliest NASCAR stock cars were usually cars with the lightest weight, such as a two-door sedan or the "businessman's coupe" with the most powerful engine available for the make. A popular entry of the day was the Oldsmobile "88" two-door model with the recently introduced overhead valve V8 engine.

While powerful cars such as the Lincoln, Cadillac and Buick were raced, they were heavy and, although the engines would last,

other parts such as suspensions, brakes and drivelines failed much of the time. They were just not designed for constant thrashing around on the rough dirt oval tracks. One of the most troublesome areas was tires. Not only were they skinny compared to today's tires but they were stock road tires, not built to withstand excessive heat build-up. Blow-outs were very common.

Some drivers, such as Lee Petty and Johnny Mantz, drove little six-cylinder Plymouths in the early years. These cars were vastly under-powered compared to the competition, but with their light weight and slow speed the cars rarely broke down, and got excellent tire wear. While all the faster cars would be getting new

tires in the pits, the Plymouth would continue to rack up the laps on the track.

In 1948 Hudson introduced its "Step-Down" model, a bulbous vehicle with a wide stance and frame rails outside the rear wheels. This car not only sat lower than others but it offered superior handling characteristics for its day, and was very rugged.

Hudson did not have a V8 engine, but Hudson had an engineering department that saw the promotional value of stock car racing. When pioneer driver Marshall Teague came knocking at Hudson's Detroit plant, engineers worked with him to build a strong, dependable automobile.

With its optional "Hornet X7" engine of 308 cubic inches and 210 horsepower, and special "export-only" suspension and brake package, the Hudson was a hard car to beat on the track in the early 1950s, with its beefed-up axles, wheels and suspension equipment.

Of course, the other manufacturers weren't going to sit around and let this six-cylinder upstart take all the prizes. Other makes of cars that raced were soon producing "export" brakes and suspensions and, given their more powerful V8 engines, Hudson's day was over by 1954.

Going against the norm of a big engine stuffed into a light car, the highly prepared Kiekhaefer Chrysler 300 team cars dominated NASCAR in 1955 and 1956. But there was a change coming in engines, a change that is still felt in today's NASCAR racing.

In 1955 Chevrolet introduced a revolutionary V8 engine for its new line of cars. Although certainly not intended for performance use, this engine was such a natural for modifications that it became *the* engine to use in racing and high-performance applications. Known as the "small-block," the Chevy engine went into every type of motorsport where a reliable performance application was needed, including NASCAR Grand National racing.

With drivers such as Herb Thomas, Chevy started winning a lot of NASCAR races, especially on the smaller ovals where this engine's high-revving capabilities and light weight were put to good use. It was overshadowed a bit by Oldsmobile and Pontiac in the late 1950s and early 1960s, but it would return to the winner's circle when it introduced a new, larger engine.

The Petty family became a dominant force in the 1960s, with its succession of Plymouths powered by the very powerful 426-cubic inch "Hemi" engine, so-named for its hemispherical

Crew members work on David Stremme's Dodge during the 2007 Dickies 500 at Texas Motor Speedway after an accident. When the car is in the garage during a race, it is not a good sign. Stremme placed 41st in the race.

combustion chambers in the cylinder heads. Cotton Owens also had great success with this powerplant. And, with its potent 427-cubic inch engine, Ford was not taking a back seat in the horsepower race.

But NASCAR thought these monster engines were getting out of hand, as the speeds of the cars had increased too much for the race tires of the day, and by the late 1960s smaller engines were mandated.

While engine development was a big factor

Ganassi Racing engine specialist Rudy Wade prepares the powerplant of Juan Pablo Montoya's Dodge before the running of the Daytona 500. The former Formula One star placed 32nd in the 500.

in NASCAR, the cars had become less and less like the "stock" cars they were to represent. The cars were still full-framed, but strengthened. The biggest brakes, wheels and suspensions were installed, along with huge radiators. Four-speed transmissions were the norm. Body-wise, the cars were now harder to tell apart than their street brethren. Bumpers were retained, but all trim and lights were removed. The glitz and space-age look of stock dashboards gave way to a home-built panel with aftermarket gauges and switches. Interiors were gutted, replaced by metal panels, a single racing seat, and roll bar protection.

Driver safety was slow to evolve. All glass except for the windshield was removed, single roll bars were replaced by cages, and padding was installed around the roll bars. There were no safety fuel cells in the early years. Eventually tire manufacturers developed racing-only tires, tires with wide profiles that could withstand high-heat, high-stress punishment, but tire failure was still common.

As the platforms of domestic cars changed between 1975 and 1990, stock cars changed in relation to Detroit's yearly model turnover. Along with controling engine size, NASCAR eventually prohibited the use of wind-cheating body styles such as the Ford Torino and the Dodge Daytona, with its streamlined nose and big wing on the rear, which became prominent, although they were naturals for the super speedway with their 200-mph plus speeds. Full-size cars such as the Ford Galaxie and the Chevrolet Impala were replaced by mid-size cars with shorter wheelbases, such as the Chevrolet Monte Carlo, Buick Regal and Ford Thunderbird.

By 1990 Detroit no longer offered any V8-powered, rear-wheel drive cars suitable as a basis for NASCAR Cup racing. While some elements such as the carburetor-fueled V8 engine, four-speed transmission and rear-wheel drive remain to this day, the cars now on speedways have little more than the name in common with today's street-driven, front-wheel drive, V6-powered sedans.

Early in the new millennium, NASCAR started to develop the basis of a new car platform that would offer greater driver safety and uniformity among the makes of cars. By 2004 prototypes were being assembled, and the various Cup teams were testing the "Car of Tomorrow" on tracks in 2006. Several 2007 events were run with the CoT cars exclusively, and the new generation of race car was ushered in for the 2008 season.

Today's NASCAR Car

The NASCAR Sprint Cup car of today blends the reliability and power of a V8 engine with a solid full frame underneath a sleek, wind-cheating body. While the cars are built under NASCAR supervision, this package, developed as the "Car of Tomorrow" and introduced to Cup racing full time in 2008, has been developed not only for close competition, but to offer the utmost in driver safety.

Engines

Powerplants are custom-made by several racing engine manufacturers with very few factory parts. Each piece of each engine is built with endurance as well as power in mind. The engine block uses special alloys to provide more strength in key areas such as the main bearings. Cylinder heads are aluminum for their light weight and their valve-porting versatility, which allows the engine to breathe better, giving it more power.

Presently there are four engines in the top levels of stock car racing, from Ford, Chevrolet, Toyota and Dodge. These engines have a displacement of 358 cubic inches and produce up to 850 horsepower, running high-octane unleaded gasoline through a carburetor. No fuel injection is allowed, and compression ratios are 12:1, much higher than a street car with a ratio of anywhere from 8:1 to 9.5:1.

All these specialized engine parts allow a Sprint Cup car engine to withstand at least 8,000 rpm for hours at a time. Engines cost upward of $60,000 each, and are hand-assembled, then run on a dynamometer, a calibration machine that gives mechanics and engineers every aspect of an engine's behavior.

The most significant — and one of the most controversial — changes to NASCAR

An engine oil fire may be a dramatic distraction in a Cup race, but it doesn't help win races. This is Kevin Lepage in the Crown Royal 500 at Richmond in 2006.

NASCAR CUP CAR SPECIFICATIONS AT A GLANCE

Eligible Models	• Chevrolet Impala SS • Dodge Charger • Ford Fusion • Toyota Camry
Years	2007–2008
Engine	Cast-iron 358 cubic inch maximum V8 configuration with aluminum cylinder heads
Horsepower	850 at 9000 rpm (may vary at restrictor plate events)
Compression Ratio	12:01
Torque	550 ft/lb at 7500 rpm
Induction	one four-barrel carburetor (Holley)
Top speed	200 mph
Transmission	four-speed manual
Fuel	Sunoco Unleaded
Front suspension	Independent coil springs with upper and lower A-frames
Rear suspension	Trailing arms, coil springs, Panhard bar
Chassis	rectangular steel tubing with integral roll cage
Body length	198.5 inches
Body width	74.0 inches
Car height	53.5 inches
Car weight	3450 pounds without driver
Front air dam	4.5 inches maximum
Gear ratios	2.90 to 6.50:1
Spoiler	NASCAR-supplied rear wing (may vary at restrictor plate races)
Wheelbase	110 inches
Wheels	15 inches by 9.5 inches, steel
Tread width	61.5 inches (maximum)
Brakes	Disc, front and rear

engines has been the use of a restrictor plate to slow down the cars. This plate is sandwiched between the carburetor and intake manifold, to control the fuel/air flow mixture into the engine.

The four barrels of a carburetor on a Cup car are covered by the restrictor plate, which, depending on the application, has hole sizes from 0.75 inches to 1.5 inches in diameter.

Plates from 0.75 inches to one inch are incremented in 1/64th of an inch segments; from one inch to 1.5 inches, the plates are incremented in 1/16th of an inch segments.

Restrictor plates became mandatory at the Talladega and Daytona super speedways in 1988, in an attempt to slow cars down after some high-speed accidents. Some believe that if restrictor plates were not used, Cup cars could achieve speeds of at least 225 mph on the larger tracks, thanks to the improved aerodynamics of the cars in the past decade.

Officials contend that restrictor plates help avoid high-speed crashes, but drivers complain that the plates cause multi-car pile-ups, as all cars are now so evenly matched as they race around the track in a tight group at 190 mph. If one car in a group loses control or blows a tire or engine, it usually causes a chain reaction and takes out other racers.

Body — Chassis

Car bodies are based on American-made passenger sedans, and have to look something like the models driven on the street. A body designation may be no more than three years old.

A NASCAR car's frame consists of round and square tubing with the roll cage being an integral part. The frame is designed in three sections: the front clip, the driver's compartment and the rear clip. The front and rear clips are collapsible, and are intended to crush upon impact. The front clip is designed to push the engine down and out of the bottom of the car rather than back into the driver's area.

The body-building process is determined by NASCAR rules and must meet many stringent tolerances as set out by NASCAR. Each car is checked by race officials with special templates at each event. Only sheet metal is allowed; no aluminum or fiberglass can be used.

When the body has been fitted to the chassis, all body parts are welded together and smoothed out into one seamless piece for better aerodynamic flow. The body is then primed, painted and lettered.

A stock car's windshield is made of a very

strong polycarbonate material called Lexan, which is used in aircraft applications. It is also a soft material, so it does not shatter if an object is thrown up into the windshield. The object tends instead to scratch, dent, or imbed itself in the windshield.

In 1994, NASCAR introduced roof flaps, a safety device designed to keep a car from becoming airborne. Previously, at high speeds, a car would fly into the air if it rotated during its spin, resulting in some horrendous crashes. The roof flaps disrupt the airflow, keeping the car close to the ground.

Through wind-tunnel testing, these two flaps are recessed into the rear area of the roof. When a car reaches an angle of significant lift, the low pressure above the flaps sucks them open. The first flap is designed to open at a 140-degree angle from a car's centerline, and the second flap at a 180-degree angle, to make sure the airflow is curtailed as the car rotates.

Fuel Tanks

Burst fuel tanks and fires were common in NASCAR's early years, resulting in driver fatalities and serious injury. Today's 17.75-gallon tanks, known as fuel cells, have built-in features minimizing ruptures and explosions.

A fuel cell is a product of aerospace technology. It consists of a metal box centered in the car's rear and anchored with four strong braces. Inside the steel outer layer is a flexible, tear-resistant bladder and foam baffling.

The foam reduces fuel sloshing around in the tank. It also cuts down the amount of air in the cell, lessening the chance of explosion. If the cell does ignite internally, the foam absorbs some of the impact. The car also has check valves that shut off the fuel supply if the engine is separated from the car. Energy management materials are placed around the fuel cell to help absorb any crash impact and lessen the chance of a cell bursting.

Kurt Busch all tucked in and ready to race. As seen in this photo, driver safety has improved greatly since the days of t-shirts, cowboy boots, and sunglasses.

Race car tires are filled with dry air, or nitrogen, not regular air as regular tires are. Compressed nitrogen contains less moisture than compressed air. As the heat builds in a tire, moisture in the tire evaporates and expands, causing the tire pressure to increase. Even a small amount of pressure difference will affect a car's handling capabilities. The use of nitrogen gives race teams more control over pressure buildup. Pressures for left side tires are usually 30 pounds per square inch, and 45 pounds per square inch for the right side of the car.

On race tracks longer than one mile, NASCAR rules require that tires contain an inner liner as a safety precaution. This inner tire, introduced by Goodyear Tire in 1966, is essentially a second tire mounted on the wheel inside the regular tire, and it allows the driver better control on the still-intact inner tire if the outer tire blows during a race.

The material used in making the tire — the compound — is different for each race track. Softer compounds provide a better grip but wear out more quickly than harder compounds. NASCAR and tire company engineers have studied compounds and determined the most suitable for each racing venue, according to track surface and abrasiveness, number of turns, and the banking degrees of those turns.

Each different racing surface and type of track requires a different compound. While tires may not look different, the tire specifications will be particular to an asphalt racing surface or a concrete surface, and the specs change according to the length of the track and the track's banking. Tires used in road course events are also different from those used on oval tracks.

Tires

Of all components on a race car, the tires are probably the most different from those on a passenger car. Race car tires are black, and have a radial design, but that's about it for similarities.

A race car tire is 11.5-inches wide, and treadless. Both of these characteristics provide more traction and grip on the paved racing surface. The tire weighs 24 pounds, about six pounds less than a street car tire. Race car tires are built exclusively for racing, cost about $390 each, and last on average about 150 miles. Between nine and 14 sets of tires will be used during a Cup event.

The Driver's Compartment

This is one area of a stock car that is totally different from your average street car. Everything inside the driver's compartment has a purpose. There are no frills or luxuries in this cocoon of roll bars, padding and painted sheet metal.

First and foremost, a stock car's interior is

constructed for safety. The roll cage is built from heavy tubing and is an integral part of the car. It can withstand severe punishment, and is a testament to the dedication of safety rules in racing. A car may be involved in a severe mishap such as hitting a retaining wall, or get jostled around with other cars, or may flip over several times. But the driver is insulated within this strong cage and usually walks away.

Other items inside the car also help keep the driver safe. The driver's seat is designed and manufactured to keep the driver from hitting anything during a crash. The seat is almost an extension of the driver, and is molded to fit his body like a glove. The seat will also absorb some of a crash's energy by bending upon impact.

Seats are formed to wrap around a driver's ribcage, and some newer seats wrap around the driver's shoulders as well. When the seat is wrapped tightly around the ribcage, it provides greater support in a crash, spreading the load over the entire ribcage rather than concentrating on a small area. As well as rib and shoulder supports, seats have head supports on their right side, giving the driver's head and neck a solid brace for going around left-handed corners for hours at a time.

The seat belt system is much more complex and robust than the unit in the average street car. The five-point harness restraint is designed to hold the driver tightly in his seat so that his movement is restricted to the motion of the car. Made of thick padded webbing, the harness attaches at a central point in the driver's lap. Two straps come down over the driver's shoulders, two come around his waist, and one comes up between his legs.

As race cars became more sophisticated over the years, window glass was taken from the car for weight and safety purposes. This allowed greater airflow into the interior, but if the car was involved in a crash, especially a roll-over, the driver's arms could flail out the door opening and be crushed. Window nets of nylon mesh webbing were mandated, and this safety device covers the driver's door window opening to keep his arms inside the car in the event of an accident.

A race car has no doors, so a driver climbs into the cockpit through the driver's window area. As he sits in his seat, he fastens the steering wheel to the collapsible steering column. The wheel is removable for his ease of entry and exit.

Inside the car, there is no padded dashboard with chrome trim and name plates. Instead, on a flat homemade panel there are several toggle switches and instruments. No keys are needed. With a flip of the ignition switch and a press on the starter button, the engine roars to life. There is also a switch for turning on a fan to cool the rear brakes when necessary, a switch to turn on the radiator fan, and a blower fan switch to bring outside air into the driver's area.

Race cars have no speedometers. The oil pressure gauge will show 70–80 psi (pounds per square inch) if the engine is running well at speed, and the oil temperature gauge will register 250°F to 270°F. Under good conditions, the water temperature gauge will read 190°F to 210°F, and, like a street car, if the gauge reads over 220°F, there's a problem in the cooling system.

A stock car does not have a fuel level gauge, but it does have a fuel pressure gauge, which is a diagnostic-type unit that shows any irregularities in fuel delivery from the fuel cell to the engine. The ideal pressure is seven or eight psi.

Other gauges include a voltmeter, which displays the car's electrical charging system, and works like a street car voltmeter. If the needle is reading only nine volts with a 12-volt battery system, then the alternator or other electrical device is faulty, and the battery will eventually go flat. Completing the gauge package is the tachometer, an instrument that displays the engine speed in revolutions per minute.

When at speed on a track, drivers use their experience and instinct about engine speed to shift gears. But with no speedometer, and speed limits imposed on entering and leaving pit road, the driver will note his RPMs to keep his speed within these limits.

Car of Tomorrow

A full set of gauges in front of the driver tell him exactly how his car is faring during a race. These analog dials, along with computer data updates from his crew, keep him thoroughly informed.

In the interests of improved driver safety and to provide a more level playing field for race teams, NASCAR has developed its latest platform for Cup cars, known as the "Car of Tomorrow" or "CoT."

The CoT is a culmination of a seven-year project developed at NASCAR's Research and Development facility. Prototypes were first tested late in 2005, and the car was extensively tested and tweaked in 2006. NASCAR officials introduced the CoT into 16 races for the 2007 Cup season, with its debut at Bristol. The new car was originally to make its full-time debut at the start of the 2009 season, but officials decided to implement the car exclusively in 2008 to avoid having two sets of rules, one for the new cars, and one for the previous cars.

At first glance, the cars appear rounder than the previous Cup cars, which were essentially based on a 40-year old chassis design. Car aerodynamics were the main focus for the new car bodies, which all share the same contour template, no matter what the make of car. The most obvious change is the implementation of an adjustable rear wing, added to provide better balance and a smoother airflow. The new car's windshield is situated at a more upright angle; the front bumper is three inches higher than before, and the adjustable front splitter directs air below the front bumper to improve downforce.

Other major changes to the car body include placing the radiator air intake below the front bumper, which will reduce overheating and provide larger crumple areas than before to enhance driver safety.

Driver Safety Improved

Several other areas have improved driver safety with the CoT. The driver's compartment now features a larger "greenhouse," with a 2.5-inch increase in roof height and a four-inch increase in cockpit width. A double frame rail on the driver's door side and steel plating on the outside of the roll cage are designed to lessen damage to the cockpit upon impact. There is now a stronger steel floorboard underneath the driver and an enclosed 360-degree steel containment tunnel for the car's drive shaft. The engine exhaust pipes have been routed through the car body so that they exit on the right side of the car, reducing cockpit heat. The CoT also has a smaller fuel cell, now 17.75-gallons rather than the older 22-gallon cell.

In an effort to work with environmental issues, the gasoline that goes into the CoT fuel cells is unleaded, a measure instituted in Cup cars in 2007, and NASCAR is exploring alternative fuel options such as ethanol.

Each race team builds a CoT with NASCAR-supplied blueprints. A completed car is then strenuously checked by officials for certification before it goes to the race track. At the NASCAR Research and Development Center, the thickness of the metal is checked, and the frame rails, chassis tubes and suspension points are scrutinized for proper locations as outlined in the blueprints. If all is compliant, the car then receives 10 radio frequency identification chips (RFIDs) to be located throughout the chassis. The data are downloaded and filed by NASCAR officials. When the car gets to the race track, NASCAR's inspection team will verify that the RFID chips are authentic and in their predetermined locations, ensuring that all cars are equal.

Mixed Reactions at First

Initial reactions to racing the CoT were not very complimentary, but as the drivers and teams sorted out the new car, the criticisms decreased.

Both Kyle Busch and Jeff Gordon were not pleased with the new car after racing in the 2007 Lenox Industrial Tools 300 at New Hampshire. "I'd like to know who it was who said this car would reduce the aero push because I could have told you from when I first drove this car that it would be worse," said Gordon at the time.

Busch was quoted as saying, "It's terrible. It's hard to drive and hard to set up."

Two-time Cup champ Tony Stewart said the car is "an engineer's dream and a crew chief and driver's nightmare," but he was curious to see "where everybody stacks up and see who's really done their homework."

But after a few races using the CoT, drivers' reactions were a little more favorable.

"As far as the racing, to me the CoT puts things back into the driver's hands more," noted Jeff Green, who had two top-10 finishes

in 2007 with the new platform. "With the CoT, even if the setup's not perfect, a driver can still make things happen and have a good run."

Veteran Kyle Petty said that more seat time would give the teams a better understanding of the new car. "It's a great move by NASCAR," Petty said about the CoT. "I think we've gotten into some headaches with it in the races that we have run, but we need to race it more and more. We need to learn it and get into a rhythm."

By the time of the 2008 Daytona 500 testing, reaction to the CoT was much more positive. "We've got more power and a bigger restrictor plate," said Greg Biffle after Daytona testing. "They punch a bigger hole in the air, more drag, but they don't pull up like the old car did."

Back-to-back (2006 and 2007) Cup champion Jimmie Johnson said he was starting to get used to the new design and liked it. "As this car sticks around, I'm more and more fond of it."

With a field of such equally based race cars, winning a race will be determined more than ever by the ability of the driver, the management of his team and the ability of his pit crew.

Body checking at Daytona. With the introduction of the Car of Tomorrow fulltime in 2008, NASCAR officials developed an entirely new set of body templates. One of these templates is sitting on a Toyota.

SAFETY

Drivers and cars are subjected to punishment that not only destroys cars but could lead to serious driver injury and death if not for the safety equipment in place on the car, on the driver, and on the race track.

Driver Equipment

A stock car driver dons several pieces of protective gear that could save his life in the event of an accident.

A racing helmet is composed of three parts: the outer shell, the outer liner and the inner liner. The outer shell is made from gel coat, special resins, carbon and substances such as Kevlar, which create an extremely hard and durable surface. The outer liner is a special foam layer in the helmet's crown, made of polystyrene or polypropylene. This layer helps absorb any shock energy that is not isolated by the outer shell. The inner liner is a form-fitting layer of a fire-retardant material of nylon, or Nomex, made by DuPont Chemical. This material does not burn, melt or support combustion. Cheek pads and chin straps on the helmet are also fireproof. The face shield is tough but pliable Lexan plastic, which is also used for Cup car windshields.

A driver's suit is made with fire-retardant material such as Proban or Nomex, which is woven into the material used to make the driving suit, gloves, socks and shoes worn

He may think they're wasting time, but Kurt Busch is waiting while officials check his Dodge in the pits after an on-track incident. Safety is paramount in NASCAR racing.

by the driver. The suits are rated in protecting drivers from second-degree burns of a gasoline fire, with time ranges between three and 40 seconds.

The latest innovation in personal driver safety is the HANS device (Head and Neck Support), developed by engineering professor Dr. Robert Hubbard and sports car racer Jim Downing. This apparatus was designed to reduce the chance of injury caused by the unrestrained movement of a driver's head during a crash. Built of carbon fiber and Kevlar, the HANS device is a semi-hard collar weighing 1.5 pounds, which is held onto the upper body by a harness worn by the driver. Two flexible tethers attach the collar to the helmet to help keep the head from snapping forward or sideways.

The HANS device was initially accepted and proven in other forms of motorsport, but not stock car racing. But that view changed with the deaths in 2000 and 2001 of NASCAR Cup drivers Adam Petty, Kenny Irwin, Tony Roper and Dale Earnhardt.

All four were killed by fractures to the base of the skull sustained when their cars slammed into a wall. Since 2002 NASCAR has mandated head and neck restraints for drivers in all its classes.

With the introduction of the Car of Tomorrow to Cup racing full time in 2008, increased driver protection has been ensured by the new design requirements.

There is a larger "greenhouse," or area for the driver, which is 2.5 inches higher and four inches wider than in previous cars. The driver is also positioned closer to the center of the car. A new double frame rail with steel plating in the driver's door area offers still more protection, along with energy-absorbing materials between the door panels and roll cage, which will cushion shocks in a collision.

Retaining Walls

All Sprint Cup tracks have one thing in common — concrete retaining walls. The walls keep the cars in the racing area, but when hit do not absorb any energy, or give, making any

After some trepidation, NASCAR mandated the HANS (head and neck restraint) which minimizes unrestrained movement of the driver's head. This device is used in most forms of autosport.

contact with them hazardous. To rectify this, energy-absorbing barriers of crushable material have been installed at tracks to dissipate the force of impact.

Presently there are several types of soft walls at race tracks.

A block of foam surrounded by polystyrene, known as Cello foam, has been used at the Lowe's Motor Speedway with good results. The PEDS, or polyethylene energy dissipation system (small polyethylene cylinders installed inside larger ones to absorb impact) is used at the Indianapolis Motors Speedway. And various tracks use the Impact Protection System (IPS), a soft wall design made of layered PVC material with an integrated honeycomb structure. The inner piece of an IPS wall is wrapped in a rubber casing. These walls are segmented and attached to the concrete walls with cables.

The newest safety walls at stock car speedways are the SAFER, or Steel and Foam Energy Reduction system. Developed by the University of Nebraska, this system comprises four steel tubes welded into 20-foot sections. The sections are bolted to the wall with hard pink foam between them and the outer concrete wall.

Of the oval tracks in NASCAR Cup competition, almost all now have the SAFER system in place. The two road courses on the Cup schedule, Watkins Glen and Infineon, present unique challenges, and the use of the SAFER wall system at these circuits is under evaluation.

PIT STOPS

Pit stops are an important and integral part of a race. An event can be won or lost in a pit stop. What was once a leisurely activity for refueling and getting new tires has turned into a series of highly disciplined skills where time and teamwork is of the essence.

When a race car comes into the pits for service, what appears to be semi-organized chaos is actually a well-rehearsed routine like no other in any sport. Moving in compete harmony, seven team members jump over the pit wall with their tools and equipment to fuel a car, change tires and perform other on-the-spot duties such as suspension adjustments.

In less than 18 seconds, the race car is back on its way. Try to get almost 18 gallons of gas,

four new tires, and the windshield cleaned in that time at your local service station!

The race pit crew is also known as the "Over-the-Wall" crew, and the members spend hours practising their roles. They work at the team's shop perfecting their craft, acquiring the speed and dexterity to get the race car serviced and back out on the track in the shortest possible time.

While the format of the modern-day NASCAR pit stop has been the same for several years, there have been changes in procedure, and most of these changes have been to enhance the safety of the crews.

Some of the newer procedures include the pushing of race cars by the over-the-wall pit

Jeff Gordon (in front) and others get attended to during the busiest time in a NASCAR Cup race. This pit stop scene is from the Kobalt Tools 500 at Atlanta.

crews. They will be able to hand push their team's car no more than three pit boxes away from their assigned pit box, the same length as the vehicles can drive through getting onto pit road.

Another new feature is that outside tires that have been removed from a vehicle during a pit stop can no longer be free-rolled from the outside of the pit box to the wall. The tires must be hand-directed to the inner half of the pit box before being released.

Here's the pit team and their duties:

Jackman

This team member is the first and last person to touch the car when in the pits. He is ready with his lightweight (35 pounds) aluminum jack and has the car's right side up in the air almost before the car comes to a complete stop. A good jackman gets the car up with 1.5 pumps on the jack lever. He then stays with the car to make sure it remains stable during the tire changes and keeps the loose tires out of the way. He also helps the rear tire changer discard the used tires. When the right side is complete, he rushes to the driver's side to perform the same duties. When all team members have completed their tasks, he lets the car down, which is a signal to the driver to exit the pits.

Gasman

This co-worker is one of a two-man team, and his duty is to manually fill the race car's fuel cell with up to 17.75 gallons of fuel. Using two containers, the gasman rams the container's spring-loaded neck into the car's fuel cell plate, which is also spring-loaded. When these connect, a vacuum is created which allows for maximum fuel flow from the container into the fuel cell. This way there is no backflow, which can happen if you're filling your regular car at the local service station, spilling gas all over your clothes and shoes.

Gas Catch Man

This team member assists the gasman by holding the first container in place on the car while the gasman readies the second container. He also operates a flap on a one-inch pipe that leads to the fuel cell in the car. When this flap is opened, air is forced out of the fuel cell so the maximum amount of fuel can be loaded. And if there is any overflow, the excess fuel will be pushed out this small pipe, which he catches in a pail. Both the gasman and the gas catchman wear fire-retardant clothing.

Tire Changers

There are two tire changers for a pit stop, one for the front tires and the other for the rear tires. When a car is in the air, the changer quickly removes the tire with incredible hand and eye coordination.

The new tires and wheels have their five lug nuts stuck on the wheel beforehand to speed up fastening them to the car. Although the changers' tools are called air guns, they operate on nitrogen rather than compressed air. As with the race car tires themselves, nitrogen is used because compressed air contains moisture, which in this case could damage the guns.

Tire Carriers

These team members not only carry the 60-pound front and rear tires and wheels to the race car but they also assist the tire changers. The carrier will help the changer in case of a stuck wheel, and the front tire carrier has time while the jackman is changing sides to clean away any debris from the front of the car. The carriers also ensure that discarded tires are laid flat on the pavement so they don't roll away into a moving race car or another team member.

POINTS SYSTEM

The points system in Sprint Cup competition may seem complicated at first, but it is a thorough and fair system that also offers bonus points throughout the season.

Every one of the 36 Cup races is worth the same number of points (except the special Bud Shootout and the All-Star races, which do not qualify). There are no "unimportant" races on the schedule, so teams must perform their best at each race, whether it is the Daytona 500 or the Sharpie 500 at Bristol.

In 2004, NASCAR officials modified the scoring system for the Cup championship, which is now known as the "Chase." The previous scoring system, in place since 1975, was altered to add more excitement and emphasis on winning races.

Officials brought in these modifications to generate more enthusiasm for the sport as the season progresses. Before 2004 a team could win the championship with consistency rather than by winning a majority of the races. The Chase, which consists of the season's 10 final races, was initially for the top 10 drivers throughout the first part of the season, but this was changed in 2007 to include the top 12 drivers. Also, any driver outside the top 10 but within 400 points of the leaders was eligible to compete in the Chase, but this was eliminated as of 2007.

All 12 drivers will have their point totals

AT&T Mobility team driver Jeff Burton winning the Series Food City 500 at Bristol early in 2008. The Virginia veteran racer picked up 185 points for winning, plus five bonus points for leading a lap.

All NASCAR Cup venues provide fans with informational scoreboards so they can keep track of their favorite hero. This is the scoring pylon at Pocono.

reset to 5,000 after the first 26 races, and each will receive a 10-point bonus for every victory they had during those first 26 races. The Chase drivers will then be "seeded" for the final 10 events based on the number of wins amassed during the regular season.

Also in 2007, NASCAR decided to award 185 points for winning a race, up from 180 points, as a second-place finisher could previously acquire the same 180 with bonus points.

Bonus points are an important part of any race and can help a driver's standings for that race. Any driver that leads any lap of a race gets five bonus points. And the driver that leads the most laps of the race gets five bonus points.

As an example, if a driver wins a race, he gets 185 points. If this driver also led at least one lap, that would give him another five points. And if he led the most laps of the race, he would get another five points, for a total of 195 points.

If a driver wins a race, but doesn't lead the most laps, he chalks up 190 points — 185 for winning and another five for leading the last lap of the race. The second-place driver could earn a maximum of 180 points — 170 points

for second place, five points for leading a lap, and five points for leading the most laps of the race. This points system is used for all Cup races, including races during the Chase.

NASCAR Cup teams were somewhat dubious about the new points format when it was instituted. But after several seasons, and with some minor adjustments, the new format has been applauded as being not only fair but giving the best performers their due. After all, the name of the game is to win races, and with this system, the more races you win, the better chance you have of getting the championship.

After each race, points are distributed as follows:

FINISH	POINTS	FINISH	POINTS	FINISH	POINTS	FINISH	POINTS
1st	185	12th	127	23rd	94	34th	61
2nd	170	13th	124	24th	91	35th	58
3rd	165	14th	121	25th	88	36th	55
4th	160	15th	118	26th	85	37th	52
5th	155	16th	115	27th	82	38th	49
6th	150	17th	112	28th	79	39th	46
7th	146	18th	109	29th	76	40th	43
8th	142	19th	106	30th	73	41st	40
9th	138	20th	103	31st	70	42nd	37
10th	134	21st	100	32nd	67	43rd	34
11th	130	22nd	97	33rd	64		

OFFICIALS

Along with all the race teams and thousands of fans at a Sprint Cup race, an important and necessary part of any race is the officiating staff.

A large team of dedicated men and women travel each week to each and every race to operate, score and officiate. There's more to running a race than just a person waving flags at the start/finish line. Dozens of officials register entrants, inspect the race cars to guarantee that they meet rulebook standards, score each competitor during the race, and make sure the track and its environs are absolutely first-rate for safe racing.

Here's a breakdown on some of the sanctioning body's duties.

All suited up at the Daytona 500, this official, along with an army of others, ensures a Cup race is a safe and fair contest for the drivers and teams.

Race Control

The heart and nerve center of a race, race control is located in a tower with a good view of the track. It is here that officials make their decisions about all aspects of the operation of a race. Race control "calls" the race, telling the flag person and corner workers when the race starts, when there's an incident on the track requiring a caution period, and monitoring all other aspects of controling the race.

This area contains some of the most sophisticated and up-to-date video and communication equipment both to keep in touch with officials around the track and ensure that every possible tool is available for a safe and objective racing program.

Scorers

The scoring team is a part of race control. This group collects data on each race car once the race begins, and records each car's progress in the race as the event progresses.

Not only is this process recorded visually with video but it relies on four methods of ensuring the utmost in reliable, honest race information.

NASCAR uses transponders, electronic buttons, manual (visual) scoring and automatic scoring. Transponders are small devices about the size of a pack of playing cars which are affixed to each car in the race. These devices constantly transmit signals to the scorers which are decoded through computer usage.

Another scoring method involves the electronic "button" system. Each competing team provides a person who activates this counting system by pushing a button every time his or her team's car crosses the track's scoring line in the race. This may be repetitious, but is a necessity and involves a great deal of concentration.

Then there's the old tried-and-true method of physically tallying each lap of a car by hand on a lap chart, a method used since the dawn of auto racing but which still has its place in today's computerized environment.

And the final scoring method, which is used as a backup procedure only if necessary, is a computer-generated program that records the progress of each race car from flag to flag for the entire race.

Inspection

Technical inspection is an important aspect of stock car racing. Starting days before the actual race, when the teams first roll into the track, inspectors, armed with special tools and equipment, check every piece of every car from engine specifications to tire sizes to body panel configuration. Through these inspections, all cars race on an equal basis. Winning cars are also "torn down" (semi-dismantled) to make sure all parts are within regulations.

THE FLAG STAND

One of auto racing's dominant images is the waving of flags for a race. In NASCAR racing, an official starter is placed in a special stand directly above the track's start/finish line. The starter, in constant radio contact with race control, administers the running of the race through the use of a set of flags. Each flag in this time-honored tradition has a specific purpose, and its meaning is universal throughout all forms of motorsport.

 GREEN: Used at the beginning of a race and at restarts. As with a green traffic light on a city street, this means the track is clear and racing may proceed.

 **YELLOW:** Denotes a caution period when the track is not clear, as deemed by race officials. The yellow flag is displayed for an accident, track debris, or unfavorable weather conditions. In most cases, cars must maintain their positions at the time this flag is displayed, and passing is not allowed. But caution laps count as real laps.

 RED: Signifies that there is a situation on the race track which is unsafe, and cars must stop as quickly as possible. This flag may appear when an incident occurs that mandates the use of safety or repair crews, if the track is blocked, or, in stock car racing, if heavy rain makes track conditions unsuitable for continuing.

WHITE: Displayed by the flagman when there is one lap remaining in a race.

 CHECKERED: Waved at the end of the race when the scheduled distance has been completed.

 BLACK: The black flag is displayed to an individual car when officials note a mechanical problem or a rules infraction. A car must enter the pits when black-flagged.

 BLACK WITH WHITE: Shown to a car that refuses to pit after several laps of black-flag racing. If the driver does not acknowledge this condition, officials cease to score for the car in question.

 BLUE WITH YELLOW: This is an information flag that is waved at a driver who is about to be overtaken by a faster car. Usually the driver of the slower car will make room to be overtaken at the first available opportunity.

 YELLOW WITH RED: Used on road courses, this flag is displayed by course workers at any given position on the course, to indicate a nearby track condition that poses a potential hazard, such as oil on the track, or a car blocking the course.

A NASCAR official throws the checkered flag to race winner Kyle Busch after he won the Travel 200 at Phoenix. Note how far the starter's stand is off the racing surface; from here he gets an unrestricted view of the race.

SETTING THE PACE WITH BRETT BODINE

Driving the pace car for a NASCAR Cup race, holding all those race-ready cars at bay, is not for the faint of heart. There are 43 professional stock car drivers ready to leap into action as soon as the green flag drops.

As the official pace car driver, Brett Bodine has the credentials to set the field in action for each of the 36 Cup races.

A native of Chemung, New York, the 48-year old Bodine participated in several levels of NASCAR competition, including almost 20 years in the sport's highest level, before taking over the pace car duties in 2004.

Before competing in Cup racing, Bodine raced in the NASCAR Modified Series in the Northeast United States in the 1980s. He also ran in the Busch Series at that time, and was series runner-up in 1986.

From 1998 to 2003 he was a full-time Cup competitor driving for team owners such as Bud Moore, Kenny Bernstein and Junior Johnson. In 1996 he bought Johnson's team and raced until 2003.

Now, during the week, Bodine works as a special project engineer in NASCAR's research and development center based in Concord, North Carolina, where he focuses primarily on cost-saving initiatives and the Car of Tomorrow. And for more than half the weekends in the year, Bodine leads the pack at the start of every race and hustles out in front of the leaders during any caution periods.

Bodine's task is not as simple as it sounds. He must be prepared at a moment's notice to get onto the track from his pit road position, accelerating enough to get in front of the leaders when the yellow flag is thrown. He is in constant radio contact with race officials, and aware of race conditions at all times. He maintains a steady pace for the competitors during the caution period, and when told by officials that the green will be displayed on the next lap, he will dive onto pit road as

Pit Road

Pit stops play an exciting and important role in stock car racing. Officials are constantly working on pit row during a race, monitoring the pit stops and enforcing the rules that govern pit stop procedures. Some items that the pit road crew monitor are the number of team members involved in a pit stop, and safety and fire hazards. They also keep a close watch for car congestion when the race cars head back to the actual race track.

Pit road officials also report to the control tower and respective team crew chiefs any potential problems they note while the car is in the pits for servicing.

Left: NASCAR invites guest celebrities to pace the Daytona 500 field in the pre-race ceremonies, and here regular pace car driver Brett Bodine is explaining some of the controls to television's Jay Leno.

the racing resumes. He never leaves his car during the event, keeping a constant vigil on the race proceedings.

While driving the pace laps, Bodine is doing more than just driving around. He maintains a constant check on the track, observing conditions for debris, parts fallen from cars, and any part of the racing surface or barrier walls that may be damaged. His eyes are the closest to the track. He is the frontline official for making sure all is safe and that the racing can continue.

Bodine also performs a service for the racers, especially on the shorter tracks where NASCAR races. His pace car has regular high-performance street tires with treads (race car tires are devoid of grooves), and while circling the track, his car can pick up small chunks of rubber left by the race cars. This non-official function results in a cleaner track for the competitors.

Aside from their special paint and graphics, and their roof lights, the pace cars Bodine drives are basically high-performance versions of stock automobiles available at a dealership. He will drive several different makes of car, including Chevrolet Corvettes and Monte Carlos, Ford Fusions or Toyota Camrys, depending on the venue.

Above: Bodine in his "office." The former Cup driver now spends more than half the weekends of the year leading the field with his pace car duties.

TRACKS

NASCAR's premier series, the Sprint Cup, comprises 36 races at 22 different tracks each year. Far from the small dirt tracks and beach races of the past, todayís races are held at state-of-the-art racing facilities ranging in track size from half a mile, such as Bristol, to the superspeedways of Daytona and Talladega, which are more than two miles in length.

While the majority of the races are run on oval-configuration tracks, there are two road racing circuits on the schedule which highlight the Cup cars and drivers in non-traditional settings.

The season kicks off with the Daytona 500 in February with what is considered to be the greatest race on the schedule, and runs almost every Sunday thereafter to the season-ending event at the Homestead-Miami Speedway in November.

When New Hampshire International Speedway owners, Bob and Gary Bahre, sold NHIS to Speedway Motorsports Incorporated for $340 million late in 2007, SMI added another track to its complement of six where NASCAR Cup races are held. Of the 36 annual Cup races, 13 will be now held at SMI-owned tracks.

The 1,100-acre New England facility, opened in 1990, has held two Cup events per season for its 92,000 fans. Now, under SMI, NHIS joins Atlanta, Bristol, Infineon, Las Vegas,

A dynamic view of the Phoenix International Raceway during the running of the Checker Auto Parts 500. This track, a mile in length, was built initially in 1964 and can hold up to 100,000 fans.

Lowes and Texas, with a combined seating capacity of 850,000.

The France family-owned International Speedway Corporation started in 1957 as the Daytona Speedway Corporation. Presently ISC owns 12 facilities, which hold 19 Cup races per season. In addition to Daytona and Talladega (bought in 1969), six ISC tracks were purchased in the 1990s, including Watkins Glen (1997) and four in 1999 (California, Homestead, Michigan and Richmond). Combined seating for these 12 tracks is 1,143,000.

That leaves three tracks on the tour not owned by SMI or ISC. Dover International in Delaware, which seats 140,000, is owned by the publicly held Dover Motorsports

Incorporated. Among other interests, such as casinos and horse-racing tracks, it owns Gateway International, Memphis Motorsports Park and the Nashville Superspeedway. Two Cup races are held at Dover.

The largest venue on the Cup schedule, in terms of seating, is Indianapolis Motor Speedway, owned by Hulman and Company. The Indiana 2.5-mile oval has permanent seating for 257,000, but this can swell up to 400,000 with infield seating for the sole annual Cup race.

Dr. Joseph and Rose Mattioli own and operate the Pocono Raceway. The Pennsylvania facility has seating for 70,000, and the Mattiolis also own South Boston Speedway in Virginia. Two Cup races are held at Pocono each season.

As part of Daytona's 50th birthday celebrations in 2008, fans were invited to sign the start-finish line of the fabled track, and this young fans adds his name to the track's history.

SPRINT CUP TRACKS AND EVENTS

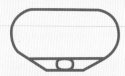

ATLANTA MOTOR SPEEDWAY

Hampton, Georgia

EVENTS: 4 and 33

TYPE: Oval

SIZE: 1.54 miles

BANKING IN CORNERS: 24°

DATE BUILT: 1959

FIRST CUP RACE: 1972

SEATING CAPACITY: 124,000

Rebuilt in 1997

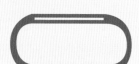

BRISTOL MOTOR SPEEDWAY

Bristol, Tennessee

EVENTS: 5 and 24

TYPE: Oval

SIZE: 0.533 miles

BANKING IN CORNERS: 36°

DATE BUILT: 1961

FIRST CUP RACE: 1972

SEATING CAPACITY: 160,000

Concrete surface

CALIFORNIA SPEEDWAY

Fontana, California

EVENTS: 2 and 25

TYPE: D-Oval

SIZE: 2.0 miles

BANKING IN CORNERS: 14°

DATE BUILT: 1997

FIRST CUP RACE: 1997

SEATING CAPACITY: 92,000

CHICAGOLAND SPEEDWAY

Joliet, Illinois

EVENTS: 19

TYPE: Trioval

SIZE: 1.5 miles

BANKING IN CORNERS: 18°

DATE BUILT: 2001

FIRST CUP RACE: 2001

SEATING CAPACITY: 75,000

DARLINGTON RACEWAY

Darlington, South Carolina

EVENTS: 11

TYPE: Oval

SIZE: 1.366 miles

BANKING IN CORNERS: 25°

DATE BUILT: 1949

FIRST CUP RACE: 1972

SEATING CAPACITY: 65,000

EVENT: Dodge Charger 500

Egg-shaped

DAYTONA INTERNATIONAL SPEEDWAY

Daytona Beach, Florida

EVENTS: 1 and 18

TYPE: Trioval

SIZE: 2.5 miles

BANKING IN CORNERS: 31°

DATE BUILT: 1959

FIRST CUP RACE: 1959

SEATING CAPACITY: 165,000

DOVER INTERNATIONAL SPEEDWAY

Dover, Delaware

EVENTS: 13 and 28

TYPE: Oval

SIZE: 1.0 miles

BANKING IN CORNERS: 24°

DATE BUILT: 1969

FIRST CUP RACE: 1972

SEATING CAPACITY: 140,000

Known as "The Monster Mile"

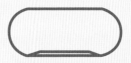

HOMESTEAD-MIAMI SPEEDWAY

Homestead, Florida

EVENTS: 36

TYPE: Oval

SIZE: 1.5 miles

BANKING IN CORNERS: 20°

DATE BUILT: 1995

FIRST CUP RACE: 1999

SEATING CAPACITY: 72,000

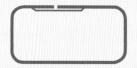

INDIANAPOLIS MOTOR SPEEDWAY

Speedway, Indiana

EVENTS: 20

TYPE: Oval

SIZE: 2.5 miles

BANKING IN CORNERS: 9°

DATE BUILT: 1909

FIRST CUP RACE: 1994

SEATING CAPACITY: 250,000

Originally paved with brick

INFINEON RACEWAY

Sonoma, California

EVENTS: 16

TYPE: Road Course

SIZE: 1.99 miles

BANKING IN CORNERS: varies

DATE BUILT: 1968

FIRST CUP RACE: 1989

SEATING CAPACITY: varies

KANSAS SPEEDWAY

Kansas City, Missouri

EVENTS: 29

TYPE: Trioval

SIZE: 1.5 miles

BANKING IN CORNERS: 15°

DATE BUILT: 2001

FIRST CUP RACE: 2001

SEATING CAPACITY: 80,000

LAS VEGAS MOTOR SPEEDWAY

Las Vegas, Nev.

EVENTS: 3

TYPE: Trioval

SIZE: 1.5 miles

BANKING IN CORNERS: 12°

DATE BUILT: 1995

FIRST CUP RACE: 1998

SEATING CAPACITY: 126,000

LOWE'S MOTOR SPEEDWAY

Concord, North Carolina

EVENTS: 12 and 31

TYPE: Quad Oval

SIZE: 1.5 miles

BANKING IN CORNERS: 24°

DATE BUILT: 1959

FIRST CUP RACE: 1972

SEATING CAPACITY: 167,000

Condo living on site

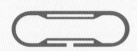

MARTINSVILLE SPEEDWAY

Martinsville, Va.

EVENTS: 6 and 32

TYPE: Oval

SIZE: 0.526 miles

BANKING IN CORNERS: 12°

DATE BUILT: 1947

FIRST CUP RACE: 1972

SEATING CAPACITY: 86,000

MICHIGAN INTERNATIONAL SPEEDWAY

Brooklyn, Michigan

EVENTS: 15 and 23

TYPE: Trioval

SIZE: 2 miles

BANKING IN CORNERS: 18°

DATE BUILT: 1968

FIRST CUP RACE: 1972

SEATING CAPACITY: 82,000

NEW HAMPSHIRE INTERNATIONAL SPEEDWAY

Loudon, New Hampshire

EVENTS: 17 and 27

TYPE: Oval

SIZE: 1.058 miles

BANKING IN CORNERS: 18°

DATE BUILT: 1968

FIRST CUP RACE: 1972

SEATING CAPACITY: 91,000

PHOENIX INTERNATIONAL RACEWAY

Avondale, Arizona

EVENTS: 8 and 35

TYPE: Oval

SIZE: 1 mile

BANKING IN CORNERS: 11°

DATE BUILT: 1964

FIRST CUP RACE: 1988

SEATING CAPACITY: 100,000

POCONO RACEWAY

Long Pond, Pennsylvania

EVENTS: 14 and 21

TYPE: Trioval

SIZE: 2.5 miles

BANKING IN CORNERS: 14°

DATE BUILT: 1968

FIRST CUP RACE: 1974

SEATING CAPACITY: 70,000

Each corner banked differently

RICHMOND INTERNATIONAL RACEWAY

Richmond, Virginia

EVENTS: 10 and 26

TYPE: Oval

SIZE: 0.75 miles

BANKING IN CORNERS: 14°

DATE BUILT: 1946

FIRST CUP RACE: 1972

SEATING CAPACITY: 105,000

First NASCAR race

TALLADEGA SUPERSPEEDWAY

Talladega, Alabama

EVENTS: 9 and 30

TYPE: Trioval

SIZE: 2.66 miles

BANKING IN CORNERS: 33°

DATE BUILT: 1969

FIRST CUP RACE: 1972

SEATING CAPACITY: 143,000

Largest track on circuit

TEXAS MOTOR SPEEDWAY

Fort Worth, Texas

EVENTS: 7 and 34

TYPE: Quad Oval

SIZE: 1.5 miles

BANKING IN CORNERS: 24°

DATE BUILT: 1997

FIRST CUP RACE: 1997

SEATING CAPACITY: 155,000

Features 194 VIP suites

WATKINS GLEN INTERNATIONAL

Watkins Glen,New York

EVENTS: 22

TYPE: Road Course

SIZE: 2.45 miles

BANKING IN CORNERS: varies

DATE BUILT: 1949

FIRST CUP RACE: 1986

SEATING CAPACITY: varies

THE BUSINESS OF NASCAR

In 1949, the first full year of NASCAR racing, Robert "Red" Byron won the championship title and about $5,800. Byron raced until 1952, had 15 starts, and won a lifetime total of $10,100.

In 2007, NASCAR Nextel Cup champ Jimmie Johnson won over $15 million.

This is a vivid demonstration of how NASCAR has grown from its rural roots to racing events that are two- and three-day extravaganzas in most of the larger U.S. urban centers.

To appreciate the financial juggernaut the NASCAR Cup series has become, consider that the California driver won over $7.3 million in point fund awards alone, adding to his race

winnings of over $7.6 million plus another $350,000 in special awards. His total for the year, according to NASCAR records, was $15,313,920. Johnson's lifetime Cup earnings are now over $59.5 million.

Each of the top 10 finishers of 2007 received over $1 million in prize money, and NASCAR distributed $32.8 million to its competitors in points fund money for 2007.

Where does this money come from?

Tickets

Over seven million fans have been buying tickets to one or more of the 36 annual NASCAR Cup races for several years now. With 23 tracks on the circuit, Darlington holds 65,000 fans,

Fans celebrate Daytona's 50th birthday in 2008.

while at the other end, Indianapolis Motor Speedway seats 275,000 fans. Of these 23 venues, 11 facilities hold more than 100,000 people.

In 1959 a spectator ticket in the Oldfield section at Daytona cost $8. Now the same seat costs about $150. If you want a premium viewing of the 500, expect to pay a premium price of $1,750 for a four-day package in the Executive Suite at the start-finish line in the Sprint Tower.

Television

In addition to fans paying at the turnstiles for the 36 races, huge sponsorships, contingency awards and product marketing rights, a lot of NASCAR's funding is provided by television coverage.

Late in 2005 the stock car series completed an eight-year deal with several broadcast media, including Fox, Turner, ABC and ESPN, starting in 2007. As examples, ABC/ESPN will air 17 races a year, costing the network $270 million, and Fox will pay $208 million for 13 events a year.

Of the $4.4 billion television deal, about 65 percent of the money will go to the race tracks themselves. The Cup teams will receive about 25 percent, and NASCAR will get about 10 percent.

A television commercial during the 1979 Daytona 500 broadcast cost between $25,000 and $30,000. The same air time now costs advertisers upward of $200,000.

Sponsorship

Corporations spend an estimated $1 billion annually on sponsorships and promotions in NASCAR Cup racing. Former title sponsor Nextel Communications signed a 10-year agreement with NASCAR in 2004 worth $750 million, which has been taken over by Sprint as title sponsor.

Cars have become very fast and very expensive rolling billboards. Of the 250 companies involved with NASCAR, 70 are Fortune 500 companies. The once-traditional automotive-related sponsorship has made way for a plethora of household consumer products with everyday names.

And this money is welcomed by the race teams, who spend an estimated $1 million per

A lone race car in practice at Lowe's Motor Speedway, with a sky behind nearly blotted out with billboards.

Craftsman Truck Series drivers Tod Bodine (30) and Johnny Benson (23) at Daytona. Started in 1994, this series has proven very popular with fans, who can relate to the Ford, General Motors, Chrysler, and Toyota pickups.

team each season for tires alone. For a race, a team can use up to 12 sets of tires, and each of these tires costs about $400 each. That adds up to over $19,000 in tires per event. The average price for a ready-to-race engine is about $60,000, and the rest of the car can cost up to $70,000.

In the early 1960s the average per-race sponsorship cost was about $200. Now it's close to $400,000, so you can see why a primary sponsorship with a race team can cost between $3 and $6 million per season.

For a primary sponsorship, the corporation gets its product name on the car's hood and quarter panels. A company logo on the car's trunk lid, known as the "TV panel" as it can be seen from the following car's television camera, can cost up to $1 million.

At the other end of the sponsorship scale, a 20-inch sticker situated on the car's sides costs a paltry $2,000 per race, but since it has to be there for each of the season's 36 races, this adds up to an annual cost of $72,000.

Revenue in the Community

The running of a NASCAR Cup race provides a terrific economic boost to the community where the track is located. Based on studies produced by the University of North

Carolina at Charlotte, Lowe's Motor Speedway generates an economic impact of more than $400 million in the surrounding three counties. According to the North Carolina Motorsports Association, the entire motorsports industry generates a $5.5 billion impact on the state of North Carolina.

The Daytona International Speedway has an annual overall economic impact of more than $1 billion. This includes the running of the Daytona 500, NASCAR's biggest, richest and most prestigious event. According to the report conducted by the Washington Economics Group, Inc. and Chuck Yaros, Daytona International Speedway and Daytona 500 Experience boast a total economic impact of $1.9 billion annually. The study also found that the speedway and the Daytona 500 Experience operations create nearly 32,000 jobs, provide more than $856 million dollars in labor income annually, and generate $155.4 million dollars annually in tax revenue to state and local governments.

Busch/Nationwide Series

While NASCAR always maintained feeder series for its Grand National and Cup events, it went to the next level with the introduction of the NASCAR Budweiser Late Model Sportsman Series in 1984. This was the evolution of NASCAR's Late Model Sportsman Division, a series of weekly regional races that went on to compete as supporting events for the Cup dates.

In 1984 the series became known as the Busch Series, named after the Budweiser-produced beer. In 2008 the series became known as the Nationwide Series, and the insurance company signed a seven-year sponsorship contract.

In the 1980s the cars were obsolete older Cup cars that used smaller-displacement V8 or V6 engines until 1995. The look of the cars in the series altered dramatically in 1989 when

NASCAR changed the rules to require that the cars look more like the Cup cars. But the series cars have shorter wheelbases and engines of 650–700 horsepower, about 50 less than a Sprint Cup car.

The series has been popular in foreign markets. NASCAR has held races with the former Busch Series cars in Mexico, starting in 2005, and in Canada, starting in 2007. When NASCAR is satisfied with the performance and implementation of the Cup Car of Tomorrow, it will begin work on a CoT for the Nationwide Series.

Craftsman Truck Series

With the advice and involvement of several off-road truck racers, a prototype NASCAR-style truck was developed in 1994, and four demonstration races were held that year. The class proved very popular, and NASCAR created the "Super Truck" series in 1995.

Several Cup teams built trucks for competition, and the series became known as the Craftsman Truck Series in 1996.

The format of Truck Series racing was quite different from the Cup and Busch series. The races were shorter, usually no longer than 150 laps, and were held on smaller oval tracks. Because of pit road constraints on the smaller tracks, NASCAR instituted a "halftime" break, when all the trucks would come into the pits for fuel and tires.

In 1997 NASCAR started to phase in regular pit stops, and a year later, the trucks competed on the larger speedways as the short-tracks were dropped. The trucks were raced as part of a NASCAR Cup weekend, but they also raced at Champ Car and IRL (Indy Racing League) events. Truck racing on road courses was dropped in 2001.

Chrysler, Ford, General Motors and Toyota are all represented in Craftsman Truck racing. They run a powerplant similar in performance to the Nationwide Series cars with an output of 650–700 horsepower, have a wheelbase of 112 inches, and weigh 3,200 pounds. Most races today are 250 miles long at the larger speedways, and 150–200 miles on the smaller ovals.

NASCAR IN CANADA

NASCAR has rarely strayed from its United States roots, but in the past five years, it has embraced the North American market with events in both Canada and Mexico.

Racing in the former Busch Series (now Nationwide) began in Mexico on the 2.5-mile Autodromo Hermanos Rodriguez in 2005, and continues to this day.

Early in its life, NASCAR races were held in Canada, which shares a long border with the United States, as well as many common economic, cultural and automotive ties.

After close to 50 years, NASCAR has taken major steps to bind these cultures. NASCAR's research into the Canadian market proved the country was viable in terms of NASCAR racing, and in 2007 not only introduced the NASCAR Canadian Tire Series, but presented an inaugural Busch Series race on the Circuit Gilles Villeneuve in Montreal.

The NASCAR Canadian Tire Series is a nationwide series and is part of NASCAR's Regional Racing, giving stock car racing in Canada a positive boost.

The inaugural NAPA Auto Parts 200 presented by Dodge for the Busch cars held on the 2.71-mile road course at Montreal was a resounding success in its first year.

Research has indicated that there are 5.8 million NASCAR fans in Canada (about a quarter of the Canadian adult population). Also, an estimated 350,000 fans in Canada have already attended a NASCAR race in the United States, while 46 percent of fans (2.7 million) say they are interested in attending a NASCAR race. The average Canadian NASCAR fan has been following the sport for roughly 10 years, and two out of three Canadian NASCAR fans (64 percent) are now taking a stronger interest in NASCAR racing.

While this new era of NASCAR has allowed Canadians to watch their heroes on home soil, there were also two NASCAR Grand National (now Sprint Cup) races in Canada.

The first of these was held on July 1, 1952, at Stamford Park in Niagara Falls on a half-mile dirt horse track. The teams ventured north in July of that year as part of a seven-race trek to Michigan, Ontario, New York and New Jersey.

The Stamford Park race was event 18 of the 34-race Grand National schedule for 1952, a 200-lapper on a track that had gained a reputation as being hard on race cars with its flat rutted surface and its board fences that could pierce through a car if broken.

And after two hours and 11 minutes, Buddy Shuman of Charlotte, North Carolina, led the 17 others to victory in his 1952 Hudson Hornet. He started eighth and was two laps ahead of number two finisher Herb Thomas, also of North Carolina and also in a Hudson. Ray Duhigg of Toledo, Ohio, took third in a 1951 Plymouth, five laps down.

In fact, the track was so rough only seven cars were running at the end, as wheels and suspensions broke on the unforgiving surface.

There were some drivers at Stamford Park making the long trek from the Southern United States to Niagara Falls who would become icons in NASCAR racing.

The Flock Brothers, Fonty and Tim, came from Atlanta. Fonty took seventh in his Henry J while Tim, who started second, got in a smash-up and placed 13th in his Hudson. The engine in Lee Petty's Plymouth gave up after 40 laps, and the North Carolina native took 16th. Others included Californian Dick Rathman, who started third in a Hudson, but blew up the engine finishing 12th, and Hershel McGriff of Oregon, who succumbed to engine failure in his 1952 Oldsmobile, taking 15th.

There was one Canadian in the field. Albert Lemieux of Montreal started the race 17th in his 1950 Meteor (the Canadian version of a Ford) and placed 10th, the best showing of a Canadian in NASCAR racing for many years.

Lee Petty was driving Oldsmobiles when he came to Canada for the country's second NASCAR GN race on the paved third-mile oval at Toronto's Canadian National Exhibition grounds on July 18, 1958. This race was part of a six-event leg of the schedule through New York, New Jersey and Ontario.

There were 19 cars for the 30th race of the 51-race schedule, a 100-lapper that was not well received by the fans, according to press reports of the day. Petty won the race, but it seems his win was not as important as the regular weekly racing.

"Lee Petty of Randleman, N.C., won the supposed high-light of last night's card — the 100-lap late model race," said a report in the *Toronto Star*.

"A few minor collisions marred the running of the 100-lapper but nothing serious and before the race was over a large part of the 9,766 customers had started to leave. The spectators, enthusiastic about the regular stock car races, seemed bored by the late model cars."

It would be interesting to see how many fans would leave a premier NASCAR race today.

Petty won the CNE race, and second was Cotton Owens of North Carolina in a Pontiac. Jim Reid of New York took third in his Ford, Shorty Rollins of Texas was fourth in a Ford, and Johnny Mackison of Pennsylvania rounded out the top five in his Mercury.

Fans who didn't leave early witnessed a historic moment in Toronto. Placing 17th after starting seventh was another Petty, Lee's son Richard. While the "King" had raced in NASCAR's Convertible division earlier in the year, racing historians claim the CNE race was the first major NASCAR event for the 21-year old rookie in a career that was as successful as any in the sporting world.

And since 1958, Canada has been waiting for its next race at the Cup level.

While NASCAR has now established a strong presence in Canada, no plans are underway to present a Cup race in Canada. There are no tracks suitable for a Cup event, and the present 38-race schedule is very tight for adding races.

Almost 30 Canadians have competed in NASCAR's top level since Montrealer Albert Lemieux raced at Stamford Park in 1952.

And for over 50 years, drivers such as Trevor Boys of Calgary, Roy Smith of Victoria, British Columbia, and Vic Parsons of Toronto have gone south to compete in the top level of stock car competition. But of all the Canadians, three stand above the rest.

From the small Southwestern Ontario town of Ailsa Craig, Earl Ross was a fixture on the short ovals. Between 1973 and 1976 Ross started in 26 Cup events, and he holds the distinction as the only Canadian to win a race in NASCAR Cup competition. Driving for Junior Johnson, Ross won the Old Dominion 500 at Martinsville in 1974 in his Chevy. He also took second in the Motorstate 400 at MIS and a third in the Delaware 500 at Pocono the same year. He also had several top-10 finishes and placed 10th in the 1974 points race.

Another Ontario driver tried his hand at the big show from 1966 to 1969. Based in Port Credit, Don Biederman entered 42 Cup races, with his best showing a seventh in the 1967 Nashville 400 in a Ron Stotten Chevy.

Biederman, an asphalt short-track driver of note, tried racing at many NASCAR venues. He placed 16th in the Motor Trend 500 on the Riverside road circuit in 1967, also for Stotter, and took a 17th spot in the 1969 Daytona 500 in a Dennis Holt Ford.

While his career in NASCAR Cup racing has been limited, road racer Ron Fellows of Toronto has been a dominant driver on NASCAR road circuits, driving for teams such as Nemecheck and DEI. Almost all Fellows' Cup races to date, since he first ran at Watkins Glen in 1995, have been on road courses.

While he has never won a Cup race, Fellows has two second-place finishes, both at the Glen, in 1999 and 2004. In 2005 he drove in two events, with an eighth-place finish at Infineon. For 2007 the road-racing ace took a 15th at Infineon, and placed fourth at Watkins Glen, driving the Bill Saunders Chevrolet.

NASCAR returned to Canada in 2007 with the running of the Napa Auto Parts 200 on the Gilles Villeneuve road circuit in Montreal. The August race was a resounding success. The Busch Series (now Nationwide) race was won by Kevin Harvick, but hometown favorite Patrick Carpentier took second.

A DAY AT THE TRACK

Attending a NASCAR race in person is an experience of sights and sounds like no other in sport. By its very nature, racing offers intense color and noise — and a fast pace. The way you get there, where you stay, what you bring with you and what you wear to the track can make a big difference your enjoyment of this great action-packed spectacle.

Simple planning can go a long way

The millions of NASCAR fans who attend events each season get to the track in one of three basic ways.

The majority of fans come to a NASCAR

race only on the scheduled race weekend, usually taking accommodation at nearby motels. These "day-trippers" either drive from their accommodation to the track in their own car, or board special shuttle services to the track.

Many fans pack up their tents and camper trailers, and stay for a few days for the racing, usually camping on the track grounds themselves. Most tracks offer excellent camping amenities, and campers either watch the race from their camping site, or sit in the stands with purchased tickets.

For the utmost in comfort and convenience, motorhome and motorcoach parking and facilities are available at NASCAR race tracks.

While fans were watching Clint Boyer win his first Cup race at New Hampshire International Raceway in September of 2007, their wagons, now empty of essential food, drink and other items for a race, stand lined-up and chained to a fence below the main grandstand.

Many of the fans who set up housekeeping with their motorhomes follow the season by attending most Cup events, and a strong camaraderie develops among them.

But no matter how you get to the track, or where you sit to watch, some simple planning and preparation are in order before you sit down in to take in the action.

Your choice of clothing on race day is the most important aspect of attending a NASCAR race. Obviously different clothing is needed for a race in New Hampshire in September than at an event at Daytona in July. Cup races are held in a wide variety of geographical locations from February to November.

Daytime temperatures for the Daytona 500 in February can range from 50 to 75 degrees, while in July it will be at least 80 degrees. At tracks such as Bristol and Lowe's, expect temperatures in the high 80s throughout the summer, while temperatures at Michigan and Pocono during the same period are cooler, as a rule.

Expect hot and dry conditions at Phoenix and Infineon, while weather at Chicagoland and Indianapolis in July and August can be very humid. By contrast, the Cup race in the mountainous region of New Hampshire can be quite cool (50 to 70 degrees) in September.

Whatever the date and location of your race, study the upcoming weather to decide whether to wear shorts and a T-shirt or a coat and sweater. Choose comfortable footwear, as a lot of walking is involved on race day. No matter what the weather, a hat is a good idea — and apply sunscreen liberally if needed.

Speaking of hats, you can wear a hat — and just about anything else — emblazoned with your favorite driver's name or team to offer your support. Most NASCAR fans come to the track ready to do battle, with their heroes pictured somewhere on their clothes or equipment. The sky's the limit for NASCAR clothing and related items, as well as apparel for every Cup team on the circuit. Although you can purchase many of these items away from a race track, the best and biggest selection is available at the midway souvenir booths at a Cup event.

While a big part of the racing experience for NASCAR fans is listening to the action on scanners, ear protection is recommended for when you're not wearing the scanner headset.

Take lots of water to drink, especially in the warmer months and locales. As the day progresses, you'll get caught up in the racing and may not be aware of the sun beating down and draining your body. If you're susceptible to sunburn, wear clothing that covers your skin. Make sure a wet towel goes with you in your cooler. Throwing it across the back of your neck can help you stay comfortable in the heat.

Do your homework and read the restrictions

Most tracks have size restrictions on cooler bags, along with restrictions on the use of other permissible items such as cameras, scanners and binoculars. It is advisable to check with the "fan" area on the website for each track you plan to attend. Some tracks, such as the Talladega Superspeedway, Texas Motor Speedway and Daytona International Speedway, have downloadable guides that give information on the particular track and its policies. All tracks have handicapped and wheelchair accessible areas, respectable washroom facilities, and first aid posts throughout their facilities.

Track owners want your stay to be a pleasant one, and they provide amenities to make sure your visit to their track is a good one.

Bus trips to NASCAR events

While NASCAR fans can watch all the exciting racing sitting at home, there's nothing like getting out to the track to experience in person the sights, sounds, and smells of live racing.

Some fans who live within a reasonable distance prefer to travel to the track on their own. For those who live close enough to one of the 22 Cup race locations, this makes for a long but exciting day.

Unfortunately, not all of us are able to do

this, so arrangements must be made for travel and lodging. Getting organized can be an overwhelming experience, especially if you're visiting a track for the first time.

But there is a great option that can take care of the logistics of traveling to the track, parking at the race facility, and booking rooms for the race weekend. This excellent alternative to many potential headaches is to take a bus trip to the races.

A few years ago, groups of NASCAR fans began organizing their own trips, which included chartering a highway-type bus and driver, booking rooms at a local motel near the track and purchasing a block of seats for the racing.

Today, several bus operators provide transportation and accommodation packages, and some cater exclusively to race fans. "Race-ready" tours are the ultimate in getting to a NASCAR race. Tour personnel are well versed

in the world of NASCAR and provide the charter group with packages offering updated information on the racing, as well as what to expect at the track in terms of amenities and sight lines.

There are other bonuses to taking a bus trip to a NASCAR event. In most cases, there is established bus parking at the tracks, and this area is closer to the track than regular vehicle parking. In case of a delay, bus tour fans can return to the bus to sit out the delay in relative comfort. And before or after the big race, bus groups often take part in tailgate parties, social time that have become very popular.

Perhaps the best part of a bus tour to a NASCAR race is enjoying the whole race experience with fellow NASCAR fans, meeting and conversing with others who share the same interests. Known as "bus bonding," this aspect of a bus trip makes for a very memorable trip.

One of the biggest thrills for **NASCAR** fans is to get an autograph of their hero. Here Jeff Gordon obliges his fans during a break at the Daytona 500.

Scanners

At a NASCAR event, just as with other major sporting events, there are some high-tech methods of getting information, such as viewing the action on large well-placed video screens that show the live action along with replays.

But unlike the case with football or baseball games, NASCAR fans don't have to second-guess what is behind a team's moves or strategies on the track. Not to mention that by the sport's very nature, the noise from the race cars makes it virtually impossible to hear the announcing staff while witnessing a NASCAR race. But that has changed in the past few years.

Portable radio scanners let fans listen to the real-time action, keeping attendees totally in the loop with the race proceedings. Most NASCAR fans have scanners that allow a total information package to complement the action on the track.

Not only can you listen to the communications between team members, such as the crew chief, driver and spotter, for every one of the 43 cars on the track, but you can also tune in to support staff conversation. And at the track you can also listen to the live radio broadcasts of a race, which can be a big help for keeping race events in order, especially if you're seated in a section of the stands away from the action.

You will hear the various two-way radio talk between the team members, so that you know at all times how the car is handling, when the car is going to pit, and who a driver is drafting with.

At a short track race, listening to three or four teams will keep you busy, while on a superspeedway you can listen to double the teams, thanks to the long distance of the track. By using a scanner at a NASCAR race, you will get a better understanding of the makeup of a race and the issues affecting it, and add a

great deal to your experience.

Scanners come in models ranging from about $90 for a level-entry unit with 100 channels up to 1,600-channel models costing $250 and up. Scanner rentals are also available at all NASCAR events, starting at $50 per day.

Scanner dealers also offer on-site frequency updates for all NASCAR frequencies at all tracks. Many fans subscribe to on-line frequency updates. These services, which cost about $20 a year, allow a scanner user to upload each venue's radio frequencies in order to be ready for listening when at the track.

For the ultimate in fan participation, small monitors with built-in scanners are available. These units start in the $400 range, but offer a variety of views, including in-camera racing. They can also be rented track-side on race day. Although their use for daytime racing can be limited, especially on a bright day, they are highly regarded for night racing.

Perhaps he's practicing, or hoping to get noticed, but a young NASCAR fans shows his racing prowess with a small slot car set, complete with Cup cars.

A unique way to view a race is provided by Cup team owner Richard Childress as he watches the 2008 Samsung 500 at Texas from a special mount on the top of RCR driver Jeff Burton's AT&T sponsored race-car hauler. Burton finished sixth.

DALE EARNHARDT, INC.

OWNER:
Teresa Earnhardt

DRIVERS:
Martin Truex Jr. (No. 1)
Mark Martin and Aric
Almirola (No. 8)
Regan Smith (No. 01)
Paul Menard (No. 15)

CREW CHIEFS:
Kevin Manion (Truex)
Tony Gibson (Martin,
Almirola)
Doug Richart (Smith)
Doug Randolph (Menard)

FIRST SEASON: 1996

CUP WINS: 24

If strength can rise out of turmoil, then Dale Earnhardt, Inc. has surely gained some muscle.

It has gained another car, too, as DEI merged with Ginn Racing in July of 2007 and inherited the No. 8 car, which features veteran icon Mark Martin on a part-time schedule. It also gained an engine development deal with Richard Childress Racing, which should reduce the number of blown motors that plagued the company for several seasons.

But it's what DEI lost that is most noticeable.

The team won only three Cup races from 2005 to 2007, after capturing 21 victories from 2000 to 2004.

In 2006 Michael Waltrip — close friend of company founder Dale Earnhardt — left DEI to lead his own team.

And in 2007 long-simmering tensions between Dale Earnhardt Jr. and his stepmother, Teresa Earnhardt, led to Earnhardt Jr.'s announcement that he was leaving DEI for rival Hendrick Motorsports.

It was reported that Earnhardt Jr., dissatisfied with declining results and engine problems, wanted 51 percent of the company so that he could take charge of re-invigorating the racing program. When that didn't work out, he left DEI and wasn't allowed to take the famous No. 8 with him to Hendrick.

"(Teresa Earnhardt) either feels too personal about the number or the rift between me and her is too personal," Earnhardt Jr. said at the time.

DEI has survived the family feud and has undertaken the kind of revitalization that Earnhardt Jr. was seeking.

Martin's willingness to share a lifetime of racing knowledge has had a positive effect on a very young team, whose top driver, Martin Truex Jr., was only in his second full season when he made the Chase in 2007. Paul Menard was a rookie in 2007 and Regan Smith a rookie in 2008. Aric Amirola, who shares Martin's ride, had only 27 Cup starts heading into the 2008 season.

The company is optimistic that Truex Jr., who had a victory and seven top-fives in 2007, has arrived as a legitimate Sprint Cup contender after winning back-to-back Busch championships.

Truex Jr. says that moving all four cars from DEI's "Garage Mahal" into the state-of-the-art 180,000 square-foot Ginn shop means, "we'll no longer have to worry about not having as many resources as other teams."

It's a radical new era for DEI, which was created in 1996 by Dale Sr. and Teresa because Dale Jr. and his brother Kerry were aspiring to big-time racing.

Earnhardt, a seven-time Cup winner and among the top three stock car drivers of all time, never raced for the team he started.

For three years the team ran a selective schedule with Robbie Gordon, Steve Park and Darrell Waltrip running a few races each.

In 1999 Park became the company's first full-time driver, with Earnhardt Jr. racing five times in the second company car, in preparation for a complete schedule in 2000.

DEI's first victory, Earnhardt Jr.'s win at Texas in April of 2000, injected a wave of confidence and momentum into the company's

Cup operation. He won twice that season, and Park won a race, kicking off a five-year stretch in which DEI had at least three victories per season.

Waltrip came aboard in 2001, to increase the outfit to three cars. Although Waltrip was carrying a monstrous 462-race winless drought, the move paid off immediately, as he won the Daytona 500, with Earnhardt Jr. second. But triumph quickly turned to tragedy when Earnhardt Sr. was killed in an accident on the final corner.

Although DEI had lost its spiritual leader,

the team continued to ring up victories, with Waltrip taking Daytona again in 2003 and Earnhardt Jr. winning the Great American Race in 2004, on the exact date his father had won his only Daytona 500.

DEI was particularly adept at restrictor-plate tracks, with great success at Daytona and Talladega, where in a nine-race stretch ending in 2006 they won six times.

Earnhardt Jr. finished third overall in 2003, DEI's first top-ten result in the points race, and he won a career-high six times in 2004.

That seemed to indicate a long rosy future, but three years of engine problems and emotional inside-fighting have forced DEI to tear down and re-invent itself.

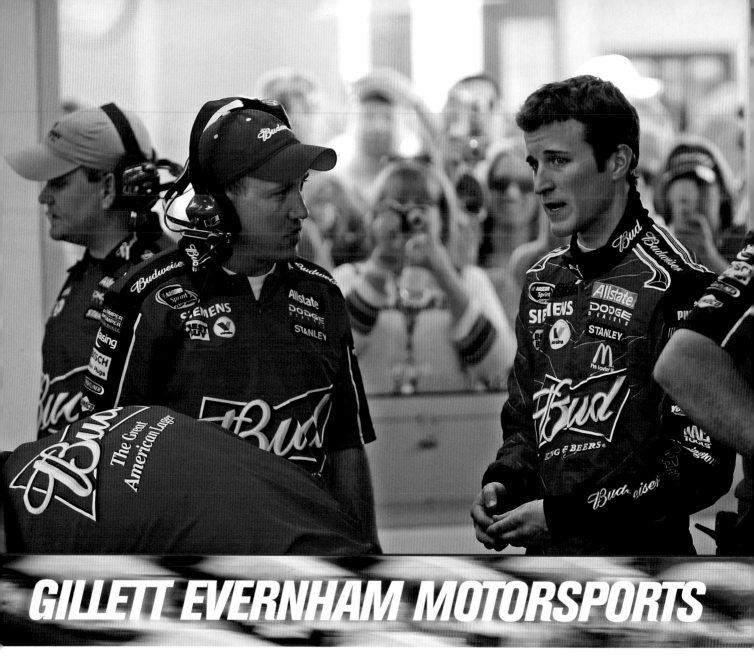

GILLETT EVERNHAM MOTORSPORTS

OWNERS:
George Gillett Jr.;
Ray Evernham

DRIVERS:
Kasey Kahne (No. 9)
Patrick Carpentier (No. 10)
Elliott Sadler (No. 19)

CREW CHIEFS:
Rodney Childers (Sadler)
Kenny Francis (Kahne)
Mike Shiplett (Carpentier)

FIRST SEASON: 2000

CAREER CUP WINS: 13

George Gillett has won over the rabid, discerning following of British soccer's Liverpool Football Club and the National Hockey League's Montreal Canadiens by making those teams better with heavy investment.

So he should be able to satisfy concerned fans of Evernham Motorsports who have watched the team lose ground in the evolving landscape of Sprint Cup racing.

"The Gillett family works on the business side, so hopefully we'll bring in more sponsorships, which will certainly help us," Gillett said after he purchased controling interest in renamed Gillett Evernham Motorsports during the 2007 season.

Indeed, the team's top two cars, piloted by Kasey Kahne and Elliott Sadler, quickly landed major international sponsors, while newcomer Patrick Carpentier, a Canadian making the transition from CART racing, is a proven fan and sponsor magnet.

Gillett says that Carpentier is a prime example of how the new partnership should work. Because they knew of his charisma and ability from CART and from his Quebec background, it was the Gillett family's influence that put Carpentier into the Busch series. But it was Evernham, the veteran of engine building and crew management, who decided Carpentier had the skills for a promotion to Sprint Cup.

Evernham had founded the team in 1999

after leaving Hendrick Motorsports, where he had three points championships and 47 Cup victories as Jeff Gordon's crew chief. With Gillett Evernham he remains as minority owner and still has strong influence on the technical and personnel side of the company.

"I felt like it was time to hand it off," he explained, speaking of the escalating costs of in Sprint Cup ownership. "I could run myself out of business, and not do a good job for Dodge and all the people who supported me. Or I could be part of this and help grow it, rather than try to control it."

As late as 2006, it seemed that Evernham's company had turned a corner and was ready to challenge the Cup's mega-teams.

In 2005 Jeremy Mayfield made the Chase (ninth overall), and both he and Kahne had victories, making 2005 the first season that more than one Evernham driver had won a race. But the team struggled with the Dodge configurations, and Kahne, who had been rookie of the year the season before, was a frustrated 23rd in the points standings.

Kahne rebounded in 2006 with a series-leading six wins, six poles and the best points race finish (eighth) in company history. The team went to a third car, with Scott Riggs finishing a respectable 20th, with eight top-10 finishes. And when Mayfield struggled, he was jettisoned in August in favor of Sadler, formerly of Robert Yates Racing.

That promising season was followed by a disaster in the opening stages of 2007 when all three crew chiefs were suspended for infractions in Daytona 500 qualifying, and the drivers were docked points. After rallying to a sixth-place finish in the Daytona 500, Kahne missed the top-10 in the next 17 races and struggled to 19th overall. Sadler was a

disappointing 25th and Riggs, who had only one top-10 finish all year, was replaced by Carpentier late in the season.

In the midst of it all, majority ownership shifted to Gillett, who had seriously considered investing in NASCAR as long ago as the mid-1970s.

Evernham has never been afraid of radical change. He left the security of a successful job with Hendrick to establish his own team, and struck a deal with Dodge, which had been absent from Cup racing for 23 years.

Casey Atwood ran three races for Evernham

in 2000, but Dodge's first full Cup season was 2001, after a brilliant 500-day countdown to the Daytona 500. It was a magnificent debut, with Bill Elliott winning the season-opening pole and presenting Evernham his first victory as an owner in the season finale at Homestead.

Elliott won four more times for Evernham and in 2004, his final season, he mentored Kahne to the rookie-of-the-year crown.

After a team-wide slide in 2005, Evernham responded by reconfiguring the way each team was managed. And in 2007 he made the hardest change of all, climbing into the back seat of the ownership car.

"We've now got the resources to compete in this business," he said.

Below: Crew members work on the radiator of one of the Gillett Evernham Motorsports Dodge Chargers during Daytona practice. The team is looking for the stability it has lacked the last several years.

Opposite: Kasey Kahne (above) and his fellow Gillett Evernham drivers hope to do better in their Dodges this season with renewed resources from George Gillett, who was brought on to help the business side of the team.

HENDRICK MOTORSPORTS

OWNER:
Rick Hendrick

DRIVERS:
Casey Mears (No. 5)
Jeff Gordon (No. 24)
Dale Earnhardt Jr. (No. 88)
Jimmie Johnson (No. 48)

CREW CHIEFS:
Alan Gustafson (Mears)
Steve Letarte (Gordon)
Tony Eury Jr. (Earnhardt)
Chad Knaus (Johnson)

FIRST SEASON: 1984

CUP WINS: 167

If this was supposed to be the era when one team could not dominate Sprint Cup racing, someone forgot to tell Rick Hendrick.

From 2004 to 2007 Hendrick Motorsports drivers won 51 times, more than one-third of all Cup races. In the magnificent 2007 season, when Hendrick spent more than any team on Car of Tomorrow development, his drivers won nine of the 16 CoT events and 18 races overall, exactly half the schedule.

Hendrick surged in front and plans to stay there.

"We can't come back just like we are," he says of the company philosophy. "You're trying to stay at least abreast or ahead of the pack.

We've really tried to look every year at our competitors and see where we're short and then improve."

How do you improve on a season in which one of your drivers, Jimmie Johnson, won his second straight points title, another of your drivers, four-time champion Jeff Gordon, finished second, and between them won six of the last seven races?

For one thing, you say goodbye to Kyle Busch, one of the bright young stars of the sport, to make room for Dale Earnhardt Jr., the most popular driver on the continent.

It's no wonder some NASCAR observers call Hendrick Motorsports the New York Yankees of Cup racing.

It doesn't hurt to have great drivers, of course. Hendrick's top three are complemented by Casey Mears who came over from Chip Ganassi Racing in 2007 and has since broken a long victory drought and had five top fives.

But while the team's strength flowers with its drivers, the roots are in its superior financial resources, a massive, confident work force and the fast, reliable engines the company constructs. In 2007 the four Hendrick cars combined for exactly one engine failure. Small wonder they led 30 percent of all laps run.

One sign of a dynasty is that it forces its major competition to regroup and seriously upgrade. Hendrick's superiority was one of the major reasons why Jack Roush and Ray Evernham brought in heavy new investment, Joe Gibbs switched manufacturers, and Richard Childress and DEI merged engine shops.

Hendrick Motorsports has found the bright light of success so frequently that it's easy to forget the dark cloud of tragedy that has so often beset the family and the company.

In 1996 Rick Hendrick was diagnosed with leukemia, which went into remission three years later.

In 2004 his legendary father, "Papa Joe" Hendrick, died and just a few weeks later, a plane crash near Martinsville claimed the lives of Hendrick's son Ricky, his brother John, and eight other people closely connected to the company.

But Hendrick Motorsports always seems to rise spectacularly from its hardest moments. On the day of the plane crash, Johnson won at Martinsville and with all of NASCAR paralyzed by grief, he won the next week too.

When Roush put all five of its drivers into the 2005 Chase and Hendrick had only one, Hendrick fine-tuned the organization and promised a bonus-sharing scheme to all employees. In 2006 Johnson won the team's first Cup title since 2001, and Gordon and Busch also made the Chase.

Hendrick started building cars when he was 14 when he and Papa Joe, a Modified racing star, constructed a drag racing car. He eventually assembled a championship boat-

racing team, then entered NASCAR full time in 1984 with Jeff Bodine as his driver. In 1986 Hendrick bucked the one-car trend with a second Cup entry piloted by Tim Richmond. Hendrick cars won nine Cup races that season and kept on winning.

Brian Vickers' Busch points championship in 2003 gave Hendrick a title in all three of NASCAR's national series.

While such luminaries as Darrell Waltrip,

Below: With aces Jeff Gordon and Jimmie Johnson, Hendrick Motorsports has won more than a third of all Cup races between 2004 and 2007.

Ricky Rudd, Ken Schrader, Terry Labonte, Todd Bodine, Ricky Craven and Kyle Busch have all been Hendrick drivers, Hendrick's biggest catch came in 1991 when he signed a 21-year-old rising open-wheel star from California.

Gordon came into a hostile Cup environment as an outsider, began winning races in his sophomore season and was a major factor in broadening NASCAR's appeal. Gordon's three championships from 1995 to 1998, sandwiched around one by Terry Labonte, gave Hendrick Motorsports an unprecedented four-year sweep.

The current all-star team is threatening to repeat or surpass that.

Opposite: Hendrick Motorsport's newest driver struck early, winning the 2008 Bud Shootout at Daytona. Here is Dale Earnhardt Jr. (center) with Rick Hendrick on the left.

JOE GIBBS RACING

OWNER: Joe Gibbs

DRIVERS:
Denny Hamlin (No. 11)
Kyle Busch (No. 18)
Tony Stewart (No. 20)

CREW CHIEFS:
Mike Ford (Hamlin)
Steve Addington (Busch)
Greg Zipadelli (Stewart)

FIRST SEASON: 1992

CUP WINS: 58

NASCAR fans try not to blink, because they might miss something interesting at Joe Gibbs Racing.

It might be their two top drivers, Tony Stewart and Denny Hamlin, ramming each other on and off the track, as they did at the 2007 Pepsi 400, forcing Joe Gibbs to interrupt his pre-season work with the Washington Redskins and fly south to mediate the dispute.

It might be winning the heated 10-week bidding war for Kyle Busch in the middle of the 2007 season.

It might be Gibbs stepping down as president and coach of the Redskins in January 2008, which should make him a more frequent visitor at the track even though his son, J.D.

Gibbs, has done an excellent job since taking over as company president in 1997.

It might be the switch to Toyota for the 2008 season after 16 years of GM products (mostly Chevys). Toyota stumbled through its debut Cup season in 2007 with no wins and just two top-five finishes. But six weeks into its first competition season with JGR, it already had a Cup win at Atlanta.

"Our goal was to be a championship contender in three years," a Toyota spokesman said. "And this puts us ahead of schedule."

Before the 2008 season a dozen JGR engineers visited the engine manufacturing plant in California and consulted with other Toyota Sprint Cup teams. By working back and forth with Toyota engineers, JGR hopes to make the engines more powerful, especially coming out of corners.

Such attention to detail, and the willingness to gamble on potential, is what helps makes Gibbs so successful. He has won the ultimate prize three times apiece in two wildly different sports: he took a trio of Super Bowls with the Washington Redskins, and has so far won three Cup points titles with Bobby Labonte (2000) and Tony Stewart (2002, 2005).

Joe and J.D. Gibbs are both astute judges of skill. They may not have the overwhelming resources of Hendrick Motorsports but their reputation in developing young talent attracts potential stars.

Joe Gibbs' first driver was Dale Jarrett, whom he hired soon after he and fellow footballer and stock car fan, Don Meredith, began planning a NASCAR team in 1991. They leased Hendrick engines and fielded their first team in 1992. Jarrett won the Daytona 500 the next year in what Gibbs still calls his greatest moment in sports.

When Jarrett left for Robert Yates Racing after the 1994 season, Gibbs pulled Labonte away from Bill Davis Racing, where his best finish had been 19th. In his first year with JGR, which now had its own engine program, Labonte won three times and was 10th in the points race. By 1999 he had worked his way up to second, and in 2000 Labonte presented Gibbs with his first points championship.

As Labonte was climbing toward his driver's title, Gibbs was first wooing Stewart away from open-wheel racing, and then orienting him in stock cars with a limited two-year Busch Series schedule for a team owned by Labonte.

Stewart was ready for Cup racing in 1999 and Gibbs expanded to a second car. Stewart responded by winning the outside pole at the Daytona 500, taking three victories, finishing fourth overall and winning rookie of the year.

He won six times in 2000 but was overshadowed by Labonte's amazingly consistent (19 top-fives) season, and points title.

After finishing second in 2001, it was Stewart's turn to win the points title in 2002.

Gibbs was already back in the NFL when Stewart won the points title again in 2005, the season JGR became a three-car team. The year before, Gibbs had stunned both the racing and football worlds when he returned to the

Below: Crew chief Greg Zipadelli speaks with his team driver, two-time champion Tony Stewart.

Redskins after a 12-year absence.

Labonte departed for Petty Enterprises at the end of the 2005 season, leaving two rookie aces, Denny Hamlin and J.J. Yeley, to back up Stewart.

Hamlin became an instant star, earning the 2006 rookie title and back-to-back berths in the Chase. Stewart uncharacteristically missed the Chase in 2006, despite five wins, but surged back to sixth overall in 2007. And while Yeley improved from 29th to 21st in 2007, he lost his ride to Busch.

That gives JGR perhaps the best trio of drivers in Sprint Cup, but perhaps among the most volatile.

Nobody blink.

Opposite: A historic moment in NASCAR Cup history. Joe Gibbs Racing celebrates its win of the Kobalt Tools 500 at Atlanta in March of 2008. It was the first Cup victory for Toyota. Driver Kyle Busch hasn't had a chance to get his helmet off as he is swamped by teammates.

RICHARD CHILDRESS RACING

OWNER:
Richard Childress

DRIVERS:
Clint Bowyer (No. 07)
Kevin Harvick (No. 29)
Jeff Burton (No. 31)

CREW CHIEFS:
Gil Martin (Bowyer)
Todd Berrier (Harvick)
Scott Miller (Burton)

FIRST SEASON: 1969

CUP WINS: 86

Richard Childress Racing is back on track. Now the famous team wants that track to lead more often to Victory Lane.

Although he lost the 2007 sweepstakes for the son of the driver who was synonymous with his team, Richard Childress found himself on the upswing.

Before his death in 2001, Dale Earnhardt captured six Cup championships for Childress. So when three RCR cars managed only five race wins from 2002 through 2005, sweeping changes had to be made.

The changes worked, but it took some time.

The climb back to elite status actually began in the middle of the winless 2004 season,

RCR's first in seven years and just its second in 22 years. Jeff Burton was brought over from Roush Racing in August that season.

In 2005 RCR was also shut out of the winner's circle, Burton had slumped to 18th, his worst finish in a decade, and a frustrated Kevin Harvick was 14th and talking about leaving the company. Childress had to make more alterations.

The company's engine program was overhauled and Bowyer and his crew chief, Gil Martin, were promoted from the second-tier Busch Series.

The revisions instilled a new spirit and sense of hope into the company, and in 2006 Harvick won five races, was in the top-five a whopping

15 times and became the first RCR driver to make the Chase.

The following year Clint Bowyer (third), Burton (7th) and Harvick (10th) all qualified for the post-season playoff. Harvick won a dramatic Dayton 500, Bowyer picked up the first victory of his career and was in contention for the driver's title most of the season. Burton's remarkable revival — he ended 2007 with six straight top-10 finishes — exemplified RCR's return to prominence.

All three drivers won a race, but only one, still a long way from challenging the dominance of Hendrick Motorsports. So, during 2007, RCR merged engine shops with Dale Earnhardt, Inc.

"Now we just have to take the next step," Harvick says.

Childress is well aware of that. He was a driver himself and started entering his own car in Cup races in 1969. He made 285 career starts, most of them in the No. 3 car, which he passed to his close friend Dale Earnhardt in the midst of the 1981 season. Earnhardt then left for a couple of seasons, but Ricky Rudd took over for two years, capturing RCR's first pole and first two victories.

Earnhardt returned in 1984 and over the next 17 years he made the No. 3 the most recognizable NASCAR vehicle of its time. Beginning in 1986 the feisty Earnhard won a stunning six Cup titles in nine years. Trading on the popularity of the car and its driver, Childress became the first owner to stylize a car's number, creating a marketing bonanza.

But tragedy struck in February, 2001, when Earnhardt was killed on the final turn of the Daytona 500. A week later, the number was changed to 29, the colors were redone and Harvick was promoted from the Busch Series to take over the ride. He went on to win rookie of the year.

"A lot of people there never got over Dale's death," one insider said, and others felt that

RCR failed to keep up with the rapid technological changes of the next four seasons.

Childress, who had run two cars since 1997, added a third team for 2002, with Harvick the only staple until Burton arrived in 2004 and Bowyer two years later. Among those who had more than 20 RCR rides in that struggling four-year stretch were Robby Gordon, Jeff Green, Steve Park, Johnny Sauter and Dave Blaney.

Meanwhile, Childress was building up the base of his company's pyramid in other divisions. He entered the Crafstman's Truck Series in its inaugural year of 1995, and won the first

Below: The Chevrolet of Childress driver Kevin Harvick gets jostled around by crew members during testing at California Speedway in Fontana.

driver's championship, with Mike Skinner at the wheel. Two years later, Skinner was the inaugural driver of the second full-time RCR Cup team.

Childress expanded into what is now the Nationwide Series with Harvick and Mike Dillon, his son-in-law. When Harvick won the 2001 Series title, doing double-duty as Earnhardt's Cup replacement, it made Childress the first owner to win a title in each of NASCAR's national divisions.

He has won 11 national series car owner championships, a NASCAR record. But now that he's stabilized his driver and crew chief roster, Childress is gunning for his first Cup championship since 1994.

Opposite: Clint Bowyer, seen here sitting between testing sessions, won his first Cup race at New Hampshire in 2007. Also in that year Childress merged engine shops with the company of his former driver, Dale Earnahrdt, Inc.

ROUSH FENWAY RACING

OWNERS:
Jack Roush;
John Henry

DRIVERS:
David Ragan (No. 6)
Greg Biffle (No. 16)
Matt Kenseth (No. 17)
Jamie McMurray (No. 26)
Carl Edwards (No. 99)

CREW CHIEFS:
Jimmy Fennig (Ragan)
Greg Erwin (Biffle)
Chip Bolin (Kenseth)
Larry Carter (McMurray)
Bob Osborne (Edwards)

FIRST SEASON: 1988

CUP WINS: 102

Jack Roush became a Sprint Cup force by developing from within. But it is an outside force that gives his talented racing stable long-term promise.

With Cup racing growing increasingly expensive, Roush sold half of Roush Racing to Fenway Sports Group in the late winter of 2007.

It is only fitting that in the very year that dominant Hendrick Motorsports started to be compared to the New York Yankees, rival Roush should align his team with John Henry, owner of the Boston Red Sox.

"We think we'll be able to close any gap," Roush said. "This is a sport of momentum."

The alliance provides extra sponsorship and the financial leverage for Roush Fenway to return to the kinds of results Roush Racing had so recently enjoyed.

While Matt Kenseth won the team's first Cup title with an ideally consistent 2003, and teammate Kurt Busch repeated the feat in 2004, Roush Racing's best season was probably the following one, when Tony Stewart won the Cup crown for Joe Gibbs.

All five of the Roush drivers made the 2005 Chase, which was then limited to 10 cars. The full house had Greg Biffle second, ascendant star Carl Edwards a surprising third, original team driver Mark Martin (now with DEI) a shocking fourth, Kenseth seventh and Busch 10th.

That quintet amassed 15 victories and 61 top-fives but the output dropped to six wins and 43 top-fives in 2006, with promising Jamie McMurray replacing the departed Busch.

While 2007 didn't seem much better on paper — or on pavement — with seven wins and 44 top-fives, Roush Fenway surged out of the season with inspiration and momentum.

Roush himself took the blame for the team's early-season struggles because he hadn't invested enough energy or resources in Ford's Car of Tomorrow. But the company eventually caught up to most of the others.

And although Kenseth struggled in the early part of the 2007 Chase, he sprinted from 12th to fourth overall by finishing in the top-five in the last five races of the year, and winning the season finale. Edwards also made the Chase while David Ragan, replacing team icon Mark Martin who wanted to race only a partial schedule, had a solid rookie season at 20th. Biffle at 14th and 17th-place McMurray were still cause for concern.

Roush Fenway continued to stretch its borders by expanding its partnership with Yates Racing, which moved into Roush headquarters in Concord, North Carolina and has access to its hardware, engineering and marketing.

That should provide a subtle advantage in the near future as Roush will be forced to drop one of its drivers when NASCAR limits teams to four cars by 2010, at the latest. The odd man out could easily land at Yates.

Roush's response to the rapidly evolving challenges of Cup racing hasn't been limited to financial agreements. He restructured the technical division by elevating Kenseth's longtime crew chief Robbie Reiser to overall general manager, so he can contribute more significantly to the other four cars.

Engineer Chip Bolin took over as crew chief for Kenseth, continuing the Roush tradition of promotion from within. Biffle and Edwards have both won Nationwide Series championships for Roush, and Biffle was also the 2000 Truck Series points winner. Some drivers reached the company via the televized Roush-run Driver X competition, commonly referred to as the Gong Show.

Roush, whose trademark is a straw hat, worked for Ford until he left in 1969 to start a company called the "Fastbacks," which designed and raced dragsters.

By 1978 he had formed Jack Roush Perform-

Below: Resplendent in their purple Crown Royal attired suits, the over the wall crew work on Jamie McMurray's Ford during the Auto Club 500.

ing Engineering, to handle his engine-building business. He then spent 14 years winning races in the Sports Car Club of America and the International Motor Sports Association.

He entered NASCAR in 1988 with Martin, who picked up Roush's first win the following season and stayed with him for 19 years and 35 Cup victories. Roush entered a second car in 1992 and a third in 1996, and by 1998 he had five on the track.

In early 2002 Roush crashed his plane into a small lake in southern Alabama — his life was saved by a retired marine, who hauled him to the surface and resuscitated him.

Six weeks later, he was back at work winning races.

Opposite: Carl Edwards wins the Auto Club 500 in California. Roush (left) congratulates Edwards.

CHIP GANASSI RACING WITH FELIX SABATES

OWNERS:
Chip Ganassi
Felix Sabates

DRIVERS:
Dario Franchitti (No. 40)
Reed Sorenson (No. 41)
Juan Pablo Montoya
(No. 42)

CREW CHIEFS:
Steve Lane (Franchitti)
Jimmy Elledge (Sorenson)
Donnie Wingo (Montoya)

FIRST SEASON: 2001

CUP WINS: 6

Former Indy 500
winner Dario
Franchitti, shown
here with crew
chief Steven Lane
at the Daytona 500,
is just one of two
former open-wheeled
champs racing for
Chip Ganassi and
Felix Sabates.

Chip Ganassi and Felix Sabates have opened the door to open-wheelers.

And in the process they've become poster boys for NASCAR's expanding mix of conventional racing history, international imports and front-page glamor.

Two of their company's three Sprint Cup drivers have won the Indy 500 and are making the difficult transition from open-wheel racing to the stressful demands of NASCAR racing. Heading into the 2008 season, third-year Cup driver Reed Sorenson was the only real oval veteran in the bunch.

And Juan Pablo Montoya is from Colombia, Dario Franchitti is a Scot of Italian heritage and Sorenson grew up in traditional stock car country, not far from the famous Atlanta Motor Speedway.

Montoya's successful switch from Formula-1 to Cup rookie of the year in 2007 emboldened Ganassi to take a second gamble on the enormously popular Franchitti, extracting the 2007 Indy 500 winner from IRL. Franchitti replaced David Stremme and, following the Montoya blueprint, was given a few warm-up oval starts at the tail end of the season.

In 2007 Montoya got the team its first Cup win in five years by capturing the checkered flag at Infineon. While his success on road courses (he also won a controversial Busch race in Mexico) could be expected, his runner-up finish at the Brickyard 400 suggests that his acclimatization to ovals is progressing quickly.

Sorenson inched ahead from 24th in his rookie year to 22nd in 2007, but his six DNFs plagued CGRFS' Dodges all season. They may have been a function of driver inexperience, which will continue with the team for a couple of years. But Ganassi has pledged to land a berth in the Chase for 2008 or 2009.

The team was formed in 2001 when Ganassi bought controling interest in SABCO from veteran owner Sabates, who had seven Cup wins under his belt. Ganassi's open-wheel drivers won a record four straight CART points championships from 1996 to 1999, the 2000 Indy 500 (Montoya) and the 2003 IRL title (Scott Dixon).

The two-car team was an immediate hit, with Sterling Marlin finishing third in the new company's debut season of 2001. Marlin led the 2002 points race for 25 weeks before an ankle injury curtailed his season. Jamie McMurray stepped in and won at Charlotte in his second career start, and won the rookie-of-the-year title with five top-fives and 13 top-10s in 2003. Ganassi added a third car with promising Casey Mears at the wheel that season.

McMurray had 23 top-10s in 2004, second highest in the Cup series, but missed the inaugural chase and after the 2005 season headed to Roush Racing.

Sorenson and Stremme, both promising drivers, came onboard full time in 2006, but there were still no wins, and the pair combined for only 14 top-10s in two years.

The victory drought lasted more than four full seasons, until Montoya replaced Mears for the 2007 season and won at Infineon. So it's no real surprise that Ganassi and Sabates turned to another successful open-wheeler for 2008.

PENSKE RACING

OWNER: Roger Penske

DRIVERS:
Kurt Busch (No. 2)
Ryan Newman (No. 12)
Sam Hornish Jr. (No. 77)

CREW CHIEFS:
Pat Tryson (Busch)
Roy McCauley (Newman)
Chris Carrier (Hornish)

FIRST SEASON: 1972

CAREER WINS: 60

Roger Penske has won several Indy 500 races, but it took 18 years for Penske Racing to win a Daytona 500. Here Penske driver Kurt Busch, team member with 2008 Daytona winner Ryan Newman, talks with his crew during testing at Phoenix.

At any track, his name resonates like rolling thunder. So when Roger Penske has an off-year in Cup racing, you know something big is coming.

The unlimited promise of 2006 shriveled into disappointing results for Penske's Ryan Newman (18th in the points standings) and for prized off-season acquisition Kurt Busch (16th).

But by the end of the 2007 season things were changing. Newman had moved up to 13th, just missing the Chase but claiming five poles, Busch had reclaimed his place among the sport's elite with a seventh-place finish and a pair of wins, Penske had installed his Indy 500 winner Sam Hornish Jr. in a pre-qualified Sprint Cup car, and knowledgeable chief Pat Tryson had arrived to inject instant chemistry into Busch's crew.

And people were speculating that Penske, after a couple of down seasons, had suddenly become Dodge's top garage.

Penske returned to a three-car entry after cutting back when venerable Rusty Wallace retired after 15 seasons and 37 wins with the stable he had helped establish in 1991.

Miller retired as president after the 2007, with 75 team wins, 95 poles and more than $90 million in earnings to show for his successful 17 years.

But Penske hadn't fared well since 2003 when Newman was sixth overall and won eight times. He and Wallace barely spoke to each other the following two years and didn't trade car information, a fatal flaw in today's Sprint Cup.

There is a much better spirit of cooperation between Busch and Newman, and Busch was the consummate team player, endorsing the transfer of his 2007 owner's points to Hornish Jr., so he didn't have to qualify for the first five races of 2008.

Penske had been a highly regarded open-wheel racer before stepping out of the cockpit to pursue his business interests. Penske Corporation, a massive transportation company that includes vehicle lease, automotive retail and tire sales, has made him among America's 200 richest people.

Penske's racing teams have won nine CART titles, three Trans-Am championships, and two apiece in USAC, Can-Am and USRRC. And Penske's drivers have won the Indy 500 a phenomenal 13 times.

"I'm hoping to give Roger a Daytona 500, a Brickyard and a Sprint Cup championship trophy," Tryson says.

Penske won his first Cup race with Mark Donohue in 1973 but ran only one full season—when Bobby Allison finished fourth in the 1976 points standings—before leaving NASCAR to concentrate on open wheel from 1981 to 1993.

The team has never won a Cup driver's points championship, but Wallace was the runner-up to Dale Earnhardt in 1993 with 10 wins and three poles. Ten years later, Newman had eight wins and 11 poles, the highest Cup total in 23 years.

Penske's fortunes then took a downturn, but with a trio of promising talent, the team appears positioned to be as competitive as the man who founded it.

Standing on the driver's door of his Roush Fenway Racing Ford, Carl Edwards celebrates his win in the Samsung 500 at Texas Motor Speedway in April of 2008. Edwards started the race in second.

GREG BIFFLE

NO. 16

BORN:
December 23, 1969

HOMETOWN:
Vancouver, Wash.

TEAM:
Roush Fenway
Racing

CAR: Ford

SPONSOR: 3M

CUP WINS: 12

CAREER EARNINGS:
$26,173,487

If statistics speak for themselves, they don't talk a language Greg Biffle likes to hear.

As the 2006 Nextel Cup season dawned, the Washington State native was favored to win the points championship. As the 2008 Sprint Cup season dawned, Biffle's numbers had dropped so sharply that he wasn't even sure he wanted to remain with Roush Fenway Racing when his contract expired at the end of the season.

When he roared to a runner-up finish in the 2005 driver's standings, a mere 35 points behind Tony Stewart, the future seemed to belong to Biffle. Two years later, that future seemed much further away, as Biffle's wins, top-fives, top-10s and ranking all declined for the second straight season.

After winning a series-high six times with 15 top-fives and 21 top-10s in his breakthrough season, Biffle dropped to 13th place, with two wins, eight top-fives and 15 top-10s in 2006. In 2007, with Roush Racing cars struggling with the Car of Tomorrow in the first half of the season, Biffle finished 14th, recording just five top-fives and 11 top-10s.

And his only victory was a controversy-marred Chase race at Kansas City.

"It's very frustrating to not be as competitive as you want to be," Biffle said in late 2007. "You've got nobody to look at but your own team. It's the cars we're building, it's the set-up

we're putting in it. We've got to get to where we're competing with the other competitors. We're a little off from them."

When Mark Martin left Roush after 19 years before the 2007 season, his crew chief Pat Tryson replaced Doug Richert on Biffle's team. Biffle continued to struggle, and with only one top-five finish in the first 15 races, Tryson had been let go.

Greg Erwin took over and things got better as Biffle compiled second-place finishes in three of the final eight races of the year. One of the top-two finishes came at a CoT race in Dover, giving the team some confidence that they could handle NASCAR's new specifications.

The controversial victory that averted the first shutout of Biffle's full-time Cup career came at Kansas Speedway, where his car was actually the third one across the finish line. Under caution, Clint Bowyer and Jimmie Johnson passed him, claiming Biffle hadn't maintained a reasonable pace when his engine began to sputter on the three-lap parade to the finish. NASCAR officials ruled against Bowyer and Johnson stating that Biffle, as the leader at the yellow flag, was the winner.

He had won twice the year before, including his third straight victory at Homestead to end the season. But 2006 had not been the year he and Roush had anticipated, as Biffle was ranked as low as 23rd in mid-April, because

Above: Biffle in the 3M sponsored Ford at the Daytona 500 with eventual winner Ryan Newman. Biffle was 10th.

Opposite: Biffle waits for his turn practice session at Las Vegas.

of finishes of 31st or lower in four of the first seven races.

Biffle did ring up a streak of seven consecutive top-10 finishes in June and July of 2006, the longest such string of his career, but he lost ground in the second half of the season to miss the Chase.

Coming after his marvelous 2005 season, the setbacks of 2006 and 2007 didn't fit the pattern of Biffle's carefully planned career arc.

Although far removed from the epicentre of stock car racing while growing up in Vancouver, Washington, Biffle caught the bug early. When he was 17 he bought his first stock car, a 1972 Ford Torino, racing it in the short, tight ovals of the Pacific Northwest.

He joined NASCAR's regional weekly racing series in 1994 and remained there for four years. Over his last two seasons he won a spectacular 54 times in 90 starts.

As he dominated the Late Models Winter Heat Series at Tucson Raceway, Biffle caught the eye of broadcaster and former Cup winner Benny Parsons. Impressed with his hard driving style, Parsons called Jack Roush, who hired Biffle to run Craftsman Trucks in 1997.

Biffle recalls that he came east with the intention of winning the Trucks title, graduating to Busch racing, then winning a Busch title to earn a ride on the Cup circuit. The plan turned out perfectly. After winning rookie of the year and snaring a rookie-record four poles, Biffle spent three more years in Trucks and won the series title in 2000.

He graduated to the Busch series the next season and was named rookie of the year, with five wins and 16 top-10 finishes. He won four more times in 2002 and, in capturing the driving title, became the first NASCAR driver to win both the Craftsman and Busch championships. He also ran seven times, without much luck, in the Cup Series.

Biffle became a full-time Cup driver in 2003 and halfway through the season took his first win, at the Pepsi 400 at Daytona. He finished 20th in the points race, and second in rookie standings.

He won twice in 2004, but finished only 17th overall. However, in 2005, after finishing only 25th in the Daytona 500, Biffle won five of the next 14 races on the way to a memorable runner-up finish in the points race.

That created massive expectations, so it's little wonder that back-to-back finishes of 13th and 14th, which would please many drivers, were not the kind of numbers Biffle wanted to see.

Biffle chats with fellow driver Jamie McMurray during Daytona 500 practice. The Washington state native started in NASCAR with trucks in 1997.

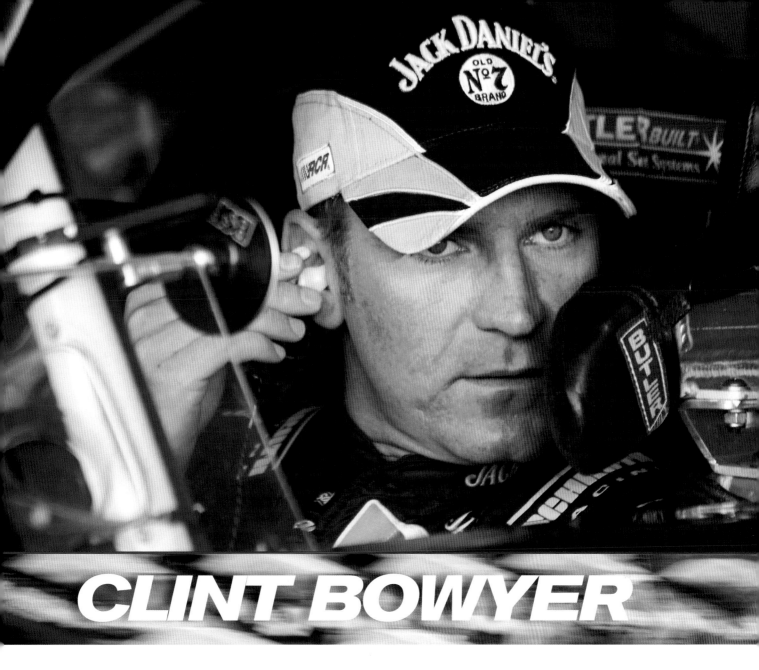

CLINT BOWYER

It has the ring of a Hollywood fable: producer discovers matinee idol serving tables in a restaurant.

To kill time during a rain delay at Watkins Glen, Richard Childress was in his trailer casually watching a televized ARCA race. He noticed an aggressive young driver in an overmatched car challenging the leaders lap after lap.

Playing a hunch, the legendary team owner tracked down the unheralded racer at his repair job in the body shop of a Ford Dealership in Emporia, Kansas, and flew him to North Carolina the next day for testing.

That was the "nowhere" Clint Bowyer came out of, to finish third in the 2007 points standings.

"It's still unbelievable to me," Bowyer says.

It was even more unbelievable to him four years earlier when he thought Childress' call was a prank and almost hung up.

"He adds that young jubilant person to our team and he's progressed really well," says Kevin Harvick, who mentored Bowyer in his first couple of seasons with RCR.

After a couple of seasons in the Busch Series, including a runner-up finish in 2005, Bowyer became a full-time Cup driver in 2006. His best finish was a third at California, but he made a solid impression with a sixth at the Daytona 500, in just his second Cup start, and finished 17th overall.

He began the 2007 season on every sports

NO: 07
BORN: May 30, 1979
HOMETOWN:
Emporia, Kan.
TEAM:
Richard Childress
Racing
CAR: Chevrolet
SPONSOR:
Jack Daniel's
CUP WINS: 1
CAREER EARNINGS:
$11,499,488

With some solid performances behind him now, Bowyer's autographs are always in demand.

news highlight reel, sliding across the Daytona 500 finish line upside-down, with flames shooting out of the windshield.

He returned to Daytona for the Pepsi 400 in the first week of July and led for 55 laps. He was in front coming off a yellow flag with 13 laps to go, but with his inexperience, got shuffled aside and finished seventh.

But it was another memorable Bowyer Daytona, as he finished seventh in the No. 7 car on 07/07/07.

Still winless, but remarkably consistent, he made the Chase as the 12th and final qualifier. But in the first race of the playoff at New Hampshire, he took the pole, led 222 of the 300 laps and came home nearly six seconds ahead of runner-up Jeff Gordon, the third-largest winning margin of the season.

It was the first victory of his fledgling career and suddenly he was no longer anonymous — no longer Childress' risky investment.

Gordon pulled alongside to offer congratulations during the victory lap, while Jimmie Johnson and Tony Stewart came to Victory Lane to welcome Bowyer to the winners' circle.

"Those are your peers," Bowyer said. "Those are the people you've looked up to in racing and those are the guys you wanted to be like three or four years ago. I would have never dreamed that I would be able to race against them."

He stayed in a three-way race for the title with Johnson and Gordon until they finished

one–two at Martinsville while he was ninth, in the sixth week of the playoff. However his third-place overall finish was a brilliant result for a sophomore who had been so recently plucked from racing obscurity.

Previous page: Former ARCA driver Bowyer impressed Richard Childress enough that he was given a try in 2003. After some Busch Series racing, he went to Cup racing, and placed third in points in 2007.

Bowyer grew up as the middle of three motocross-crazy brothers in Emporia. They honed their love of speed and danger by driving bicycles off a ramp into the local lake.

His father owned a towing business, and well before he was a teenager Bowyer was tinkering with the wrecks his father would bring home. To this day, he's still a classic car buff. His parents, Chris and Jana, sold a couple of their own vintage cars to help finance the racing aspirations of their three growing sons.

Bowyer started racing motocross when he was five and won more than 200 races before he switched to stock cars in 1996 at the age of 17.

"I was getting tired of the grind and wanted a new challenge," he explains.

He began competing at Thunderhill Speedway in Mayetta, Kansas, won the Modified championship there in 2000 and the next year won 18 times in 40 starts to capture the Modified title at Lakeside Speedway and Lakeland Park.

In 2002 he won the titles in Modified at Lakeside and Late Models at I-70 Speedway, which gave him the NASCAR Weekly Racing Series mid-western championship.

In August of 2003, Bowyer and his father found an old ARCA car in North Carolina and entered it in a race in Nashville. A few hundred miles to the north, a famous NASCAR owner was just turning on his television set.

Within a few months, Bowyer was sharing Busch Series driving duties with Kevin Harvick and his rapid ascent had begun.

"It's just incredible to even be a part of the Cup series," Bowyer said. "It's an honor and a privilege and it's something I owe Richard Childress a lot for."

Bowyer mixes it up in the Bud Shootout with Kurt Busch (2) and Michael Waltrip (55).

JEFF BURTON

NO: 31

BORN: June 29, 1967

HOMETOWN:
South Boston, Va.

TEAM:
Richard Childress
Racing

CAR: Chevrolet

SPONSOR:
AT&T Mobility

CUP WINS: 19

CAREER EARNINGS:
$54,345,624

It took some time, and a lot of movement, but Jeff Burton's career is right back on track.

Some insiders, including Burton himself, might argue that the popular veteran had never left the rails, but there can be no doubt that his 2006 and 2007 seasons constituted a major turnaround.

In a remarkably consistent five-year run that ended in 2001, Burton recorded 17 victories, had 72 top-five results, never finished out of the top 10 in the points standings and was regarded as one of NASCAR's elite drivers.

Then over the next four years, he managed not a single win, had only 13 top-five finishes, was ranked 12th twice and 18th twice, and in the middle of the 2004 season was transferred from Roush Racing to Richard Childress Racing.

They were down times, but the resurrection came in Burton's second full season with RCR, just as it had in his second full season with Roush, back in 1997 when he recorded the first three victories of his career.

His improvement started in the second-tier Busch Series, where he captured two victories, ending a four-year streak in which he didn't win in any series.

In Cup racing, with new crew chief Scott Miller and sweeping adjustments at RCR, Burton qualified for the Chase in 2006, won at Dover in late September to break a 175-race

drought and slip into first place in the points race for four weeks. He took four poles, his first inside front row starts in four years, and eventually finished seventh overall.

To prove it was no fluke, he won at Texas in early 2007, becoming the first repeat victor at the track where he had been the inaugural winner 10 years earlier. He qualified for the Chase again and finished tied for seventh.

Over the two-year rebound, he had 16 top-five Cup finishes, not to mention seven Busch Series victories.

Burton was back, but not satisfied.

"It's a great thing to make the Chase," Burton said at the end of the '07 season. "But we're here to contend for championships and we

didn't do that in a year when I thought we could, so we're disappointed."

Burton said that the RCR cars need "just a little more speed. We've got to find a way to lead more laps and win more races."

And when Burton talks people tend to listen. They always have, which is why he's considering running for the Virginia state senate after his racing career ends.

His arguments are always well presented and he's become the unofficial spokesman for Cup drivers, particularly on safety issues. When *NASCAR Illustrated* selected him as its Person of the Year for 2007, the announcement read, in part: "His words reach every corner of the NASCAR universe."

Above: Burton gets his Chevrolet serviced during the Food City 500 at Bristol.

Opposite: Burton got into a stock car in 1984 and hasn't looked back. He has had an up-and-down Cup career, and now races with Richard Childress.

He is so well regarded that when his car lost sponsorship for 2004, Roush committed to financing the season himself. "I wasn't going to be the guy who put Jeff Burton out of racing," Roush said. And when Burton had a chance to join RCR later that summer, Roush didn't stand in his way.

Burton has earned that respect in a long career that began when he followed his older brother Ward into go-karts at the age of seven. After two Virginia state titles and four runner-up finishes, he moved into stock cars in 1984, when he was 17.

In 1988 he had improved enough to be voted the most popular driver at South Boston Speedway and win seven of the 21 Late Model features. He also started driving Busch Series races in a car owned by his father, John, capturing his first win at Martinsville in 1990. He finished 12th in the Busch points standings in both 1991 and 1992, and in 1993 he made his Cup debut with an unspectacular 37th place finish at New Hampshire.

Stavola Brothers Racing liked his promise and signed him for the next two Cup seasons and he was named 1994 rookie of the year, over his older brother Ward.

Roush signed him for the 1996 season and he jumped from the previous year's 32nd place finish to 13th, but still didn't have a win in his 90 Cup races.

That goose egg was smashed in his second year with Roush, when he won three times, to kick off a brilliant five-year stretch when he won at least twice every season, and four times finished among the top five in the points race.

The test now for Burton, coming off two straight seventh-place points finishes, will be to maintain his rediscovered form within the new CoT playing field. By late April of 2008, Burton showed he would have no trouble, and was leading the Sprint Cup points standings.

Burton and crew celebrate a long-overdue win, this at the Food City 500 at Bristol in March of 2008. He started in eighth.

KURT BUSCH

Tony Stewart was able to do it, and so was Rusty Wallace, the legend Kurt Busch replaced in the No. 2 Dodge.

Now Busch is doing his best to make the transition from villain to good guy in the minds of NASCAR's massive fan base.

For his first six seasons of Cup racing, Busch seemed to have had one well-publicized bad encounter after another, including one with the police in the dark days of his exit from Roush Racing.

But since arriving at Penske Racing for the 2006 Cup season Busch has become, if not the King of Kindness then certainly a member of that royal family.

For instance, when Penske brought Sam Hornish Jr. over from its IRL division to Sprint Cup, Busch agreed to have his owner's points transferred to Hornish so the rookie wouldn't have to depend upon qualifying in early 2008.

Busch had provisional qualifying spots available because of his 2004 Cup title, but it still meant that early in the season he and his crew would not enjoy the prime garage spots they had earned.

"It's a win-win situation and I'm a team player," Busch explained.

That had not always been the case. But Busch has clearly learned from his mercurial days at Roush Racing, when a quick promotion to the Cup circuit might have been too much too soon. He drove extremely well for Roush but

NO: 2
BORN: August 4, 1978
HOMETOWN:
Las Vegas, Nev.
TEAM:
Penske Racing
CAR: Dodge
SPONSOR: Miller Lite
CUP WINS: 17
CAREER EARNINGS:
$43,046,288

Above: The Penske crew goes to work on Busch's Dodge in the Daytona 500. He placed second.

Previous page: Busch has started to mellow. The maturity of the Nevada racer has now caught up with his racing talent.

Busch is the first to admit that his talent was outracing his maturity.

Busch has found a comfort level with Penske and in particular with his crew chief Pat Tryson, who arrived well into the 2007 season after his pairing with Greg Biffle at Roush did not gel.

Busch had also been struggling to find the right chemistry with his crew chiefs, but six weeks after Tryson arrived he won at Pocono for his first victory in 51 races. The grateful driver quipped that he was going to rename his car the PT Special.

"I'm like a newborn kid again," Busch said. "And it's all due to Pat Tryson."

He won again two weeks later at Michigan, solidifying a rapid climb to a Chase berth, and he finished the playoff seventh overall.

"We came up just a bit shy, but overall just a great season for us," Busch reflected after finishing second in 2007's final race. "Seventh is a nice feather in the cap."

Which is a lot better than a boot in the butt, which Roush had given him in November 2005, two races before his tenure there was to come to an end anyway. He had been belligerent with a traffic officer after being stopped near Phoenix (for which he later served 50 hours of community service), and Roush officials said they were "embarrassed."

Busch was already bound for Penske, and his new owner strongly supported him, but also let him know that better decorum was expected.

He had been walking a thin line with fans since Jimmy Spencer reached into Busch's car and punched him after being run into the wall during a 2003 race. And after the first race of the 2005 Chase, Busch verbally confronted Scott Riggs' crew chief. Those weren't his only confrontations, and at one point a major American magazine rated Busch the third most hated man in sports.

Busch vowed to turn things around, and by the time he and his younger brother Kyle

prominent short-track driver in Las Vegas.

He started racing Dwarf cars at 14, and won Nevada rookie of the year two years later. At 18 he was Hobby Stock Champion at Las Vegas Speedway Park and also Legends rookie of the year.

He won another top rookie title in NASCAR's Southwest Series. And in 1999, at the age of 21, he became the youngest driver ever to win NASCAR's Southwest Series championship. That earned Busch an entry into Roush Racing's "Gong Show," through which he qualified for a ride in the 2000 Craftsman Truck Series.

Busch won four truck races and finished second in the points championship, prompting Jack Roush to elevate him directly to Cup racing in 2001, over more experienced drivers.

After finishing 27th in his rookie season, Busch's innate talent became apparent with eight wins over the next two years, and overall finishes of third and eleventh.

In 2004 Busch won three times, but consistently good finishes earned him his first points championship. When his fiery term at Roush ended in 2005, he had amassed 14 wins in the previous five years.

Busch started 2008 on the right foot as he almost won for Penske at the 2008 Daytona 500, finishing second to teammate Ryan Newman.

had a wreck — and a family spat — during the 2007 All-Star Classic, most racing people sympathized with the older brother.

Kurt blazed the career path for Kyle, starting to work at the age of eight in the garage owned by their father, Tom, a mechanic and

It's the Busch brothers leading the field at Las Vegas. Kurt is on the inside with brother Kyle in the M&Ms Toyota beside him during the 2008 UAW-Dodge 400. Kyle was 11th, Kurt way back in 38th.

KYLE BUSCH

NO: 18

BORN: May 2, 1985

HOMETOWN:
Las Vegas, Nev.

TEAM:
Joe Gibbs Racing

CAR: Toyota

SPONSOR:
M&M's/Interstate

CUP WINS: 4

CAREER EARNINGS:
$17,677,395

His aggressive driving style is designed to make things happen, so it's little wonder that so much has happened in such a short time for Kyle Busch.

Well before his 23rd birthday, Busch had become the youngest driver ever to win a Cup race; had taken the inaugural checkered flag in NASCAR's new prototype car; had joined the third different legendary organization of his career; and had driven a new manufacturer's car to the fastest time in pre-season testing.

He'd also engaged in, and moved on from, a nasty crash-induced spat with his older brother.

And that's just a small sample of the fast-track career of the younger Cup racing brother of the fast-track Busch family.

When Hendrick Motorsports won the high stakes bidding war for Dale Earnhardt Jr. in the middle of the company's sensational 2007 Cup season, someone had to make room for the son of a legend. That someone turned out to be Kyle Busch.

Busch, who had been with Hendrick for three seasons, had not yet signed a new contract and found himself out in the cold and into free agency. But the market turned hot for the precocious young start, and after 10 weeks Busch signed a deal with Joe Gibbs Racing, to take effect after the 2007 season.

His final few months at Hendrick were anything but a lame-duck period, as Busch flew to his second consecutive Chase

appearance and a fifth-place finish overall, the best result of his career.

He had only one victory in 2007, but it was a NASCAR milestone. He beat Jeff Burton in a clean sprint to the finish line at Bristol in the first official Car of Tomorrow Cup race.

The competitive atmosphere wasn't quite so gentlemanly a few weeks later when Busch tried to pass his older brother on the inside at the All-Star Challenge. For the first time in the nearly three years of their Cup rivalry, the brothers wrecked.

It took them four days to get over their anger with each other.

"I think he realized that, and I hope it helps him — wrecking with his brother — that he can mature in a stronger fashion and a quicker fashion," Kurt Busch said.

All this occurred before Busch was the odd man out at Hendrick Motorsports when Earnhardt agreed to become garage mates with Cup champions Jimmie Johnson and Jeff Gordon.

"I never quite fit in," Busch told ESPN at the time. "Jeff and Jimmie never seemed to have a hair out of place."

The way he handled himself the rest of the season, including five top-five finishes in the Chase, impressed the racing fraternity. But long before that, JGR stars Tony Stewart and Denny Hamlin had endorsed team president J.D. Gibbs' bid for Busch.

The new signing paid off in Busch's first

Above: Toyota Camry driver Kyle Busch leads Chevy driver Jeff Gordon in the Kobalt Tools 500 at Atlanta in March of 2008. Busch won the race. Gordon started on the pole and finished fifth.

Opposite: Kyle, the younger of the Busch brothers, was the youngest driver to ever win a Cup race. He is now in the Joe Gibbs Racing stable with Tony Stewart.

official week on the track for his new bosses. After driving Chevrolets at Hendrick, he coaxed his Toyota Camry to the fastest time in the three days of Daytona's 2008 pre-season testing.

"It's been a big deal to be able to come out here and run strong," Busch said. "I guess it's weird seeing me out here in a brown and yellow suit. It will take a little bit of getting used to."

It's been hard to get used to anything in Busch's career, because things have usually changed so quickly for him.

After watching his brother tear up Nevada Desert tracks, Busch took up Legends Car racing at the age of 13, often using the same vehicles Kurt had. When he left for Late Models three years later, he'd won 65 times.

In 2001, the year he turned 16, Busch won 10 races at Las Vegas Motor Speedway. He also joined Kurt at Roush Racing, taking the wheel for a pair of top-10 finishes in six Craftsman Truck Series races.

A year too young for NASCAR's new

minimum-age of 18, Busch spent 2002 in ASA, finishing 10th. But when he returned to NASCAR, he signed with Hendrick instead of Roush.

He finished second in his Busch Series debut at Lowe's in 2003 and in 2004 won five times, finishing second to Martin Truex Jr. in the rookie standings.

Busch took Cup rookie-of-the year honors in 2005, winning his first pole when he was still 19, finishing 20th overall and winning two autumn races. His victory at California made him the youngest Cup winner ever, and his older brother was waiting for him in Victory Lane so they could celebrate together.

He might have finished higher in the standings but wrecked far too often, as his ultra-competitiveness sometimes blurred the line between knowing when to push for the victory and when to merely take what the car would give him.

After his second straight Chase berth in 2007, the bar was set even higher for Busch at Joe Gibbs Racing, and with something to prove to Hendrick Motorsports, he opened 2008 by finishing fourth in the Daytona 500.

The smoke hasn't cleared yet from his victory doughnuts, but Busch is out of the car celebrating his Kobalt Tools 500 win at Atlanta in March of 2008.

DALE EARNHARDT JR.

From 2005 to 2007, Dale Earnhardt Jr. won two races – compared to six in 2004 – he missed the Chase twice and had more blown engines than a wreck-'em race.

And still, Dale Earnhardt Jr. was bigger news than ever.

The spotlight focuses on Earnhardt Jr. the way NASA focuses on a space shuttle. Everything he does or says is of interest — and for good reason. His bloodlines are among the deepest in the sport and, as with so many royal families, great fortune has been mixed with tragedy and intrigue.

But at the dawning of the 2008 season, for the millions of viciously loyal Earnhardt fans who had purchased every bit of No. 8 Budweiser memorabilia on the market, there was some serious emotional and financial re-investing to do.

Earnhardt Jr. was no longer with the company his legendary late father had founded. He had moved to a new team (Hendrick Motorsports), a new sponsor (Mountain Dew AMP/National Guard) and a new number (No. 88). While his new number has been carried by some of the greatest names in the sport, including Bobby and Donnie Allison, Buddy Baker and Dale Jarrett, it still takes some getting used to.

"It's like going to a new school, making new friends," Earnhardt said.

NO: 88

BORN:
October 10, 1974

HOMETOWN:
Kannapolis, N.C.

TEAM:
Hendrick Motorsports

CAR: Chevrolet

SPONSOR:
Mountain Dew AMP/National Guard

CUP WINS: 17

CAREER EARNINGS:
$48,903,000

Previous page: In a sport with stars and superstars, Dale Earnhardt Jr.'s star shines brightest. His new teammates at Hendrick Motorsport include Jimmie Johnson and Jeff Gordon.

Below: Gone is the familiar red No. 8 Chevy, as Jr. now pilots a green and white Chevy with an extra number 8 on it. He is seen here in his new car beside teammate Jeff Gordon at Atlanta in March of 2008.

Relationships at Dale Earnhardt, Inc. had turned sour by May 2007, when Earnhardt announced he'd be leaving the company, unable to hammer out a new deal with owner Teresa Earnhardt, his father's widow.

After a high-profile bidding war, Earnhardt signed in June with the most dominant team in the sport, joining Jeff Gordon and Jimmie Johnson, who between them have six Cup titles.

For his part, Earnhardt wanted to stay with Chevrolet, have access to a wider range of human and financial resources, and provide a better working environment for his crew chief and cousin, Tony Eury Jr., who accompanied him on the move. All of this was possible at Hendrick.

"It's a new chapter for me and I couldn't be anticipating it more," Earnhardt said.

Earnhardt Jr. was disappointed, and bitter, that he could not bring the No. 8 with him to Hendrick. But Teresa Earnhardt reportedly wanted commissions on merchandise sales and, he implied, it was simply better to be free of all DEI connections.

Because of the charisma of the family name, Earnhardt's departure from DEI transcended the racing world and was followed closely by every major news outlet on the continent.

Everyone knew of Dale Earnhardt Sr.'s death in a crash at the end of the 2001 Daytona 500, just as his longtime friend and protegé Michael Waltrip was winning his first Winston Cup race, with Dale Jr. finishing second. And everyone knew that only five months later Dale Jr. won the Pepsi 400 on the very track where his father had perished. And everyone knew of the tearful, storybook finish to the 2004 Daytona 500, which Dale Jr. won for the first time, six years to the day after his father's first victory in the sport's most prestigious event.

The racing world had been tracking Earnhardt Jr. since he could walk. 'Little E,' his brother Kerry and their sister Kelly all raced against each other when they were young.

Earnhardt Jr. began street stock racing when he was 17, won three NASCAR Late Model features between 1994 and 1996, and by 1998 drove full time on the Busch Series.

He won the Busch driver's title in both 1998 and 1999, the only two seasons he committed

full time to the series. That made the Earnhardts the first three-generation NASCAR champions. And when he, Kerry and Dale Sr. all started in the 2000 Pepsi 400 at Michigan, they joined Lee, Richard and Maurice Petty as the only father-and-two-sons combinations to compete in the same Cup race.

When he graduated to full-time Cup racing in 2000, Earnhardt Jr. made an immediate impact, attracting heavy long-term sponsorship from Budweiser and matching Davey Allison's rookie record of two wins in his first 16 appearances. And in each of his first five seasons on NASCAR's top circuit he won at least two races.

In 2003 he finished third overall and in 2004 he won the Gatorade 125, the Busch race and the 500 during a memorable Speedweek at Daytona, and had six victories overall, with two of them coming during the Cup's first Chase. But three low finishes in the Chase dropped

him to fifth place overall and foreshadowed the low finish and engine troubles that would plague his final three seasons at DEI.

In 2005 he won just a single race, was not even close to qualifying for the Chase, and was ranked a career-low 19th. He also won just once in 2006, although he did finish fifth in the points race.

In 2007, for the first time as full-time Cup racer, Earnhardt Jr. did not win a race. His major downfall was seven blown engines. He missed the Chase for the second time in three seasons, was ranked 16th overall and in his final seven races in a DEI car, never placed higher than 14th.

It was not the fairy tale end to an era for which Earnhardt and his legions of fans had longed, but he remained philosophical.

"Even in the situations that are sometimes pointless," he said, "if we continue to try really hard, it can show the integrity we have."

Jr. gets the treatment in the Food City 500 at Bristol, March 2008. He finished second.

CARL EDWARDS

NO: 99

BORN:
August 15, 1979

HOMETOWN:
Columbia, Mo.

TEAM:
Roush Fenway
Racing

CAR: Ford

SPONSOR:
Office Depot

CUP WINS: 7

CAREER EARNINGS:
$19,723,210

Nice guys are supposed to finish last, but Carl Edwards doesn't.

The ever-smiling driver from the Show Me state may have endured somewhat of a sophomore slump in 2006 but he came back swinging, and not just metaphorically.

After being blanked for an entire campaign following his spectacular full-season debut in 2005, Edwards re-established himself in 2007, winning three times, qualifying for the Chase and dominating the second-tier Busch Series.

And he also challenged his mild-mannered image with an aggressive late-season confrontation with Roush-Fenway teammate Matt Kenseth.

Edwards apologized immediately but was shocked at the aftermath, when the incident was discussed at high pitch for several days. The video of their argument was plastered all over the Internet, and a few fellow drivers made negative comments.

In the long run, though, it will be regarded as just another part of Edwards' fast-track education on racing's biggest stage

"I learned a little bit about perspective," Edwards later said of the incident at Martinsville, where he pushed Kenseth, then faked a punch. "The bottom line is this is an entertainment sport. It has competition and there are going to be times where it doesn't go as you want. The bottom line is, if it wasn't something

you got wound up about every now and then, it wouldn't be worth doing."

His 2007 season was certainly worth doing.

His win at Michigan in June broke a 52-week winless drought stretching back to late 2005: his debut season in which he won four times and finished third in the Nextel Cup standings. But he finished 12th overall in 2006, missed the Chase, and didn't win a race, partly because owner Jack Roush had shifted crew chief Bob Osborne to Jamie McMurray, hoping to ease McMurray's transition into his new team.

"I went from hero to zero," Edwards quipped.

Roush realized his mistake, and Osborne and Edwards were reunited for 2007. The partnership clicked again, and Edwards picked up his second victory of the season in late August, winning decisively at Bristol. That clinched his berth in the Chase and was also Ford's first victory in NASCAR's Car of Tomorrow.

Edwards won the second race of the Chase, a record 13-caution crash-a-thon at Dover, but his car was measured more than a half-inch lower than standard and failed the post-race inspection. He kept the win but was assessed a 25-point penalty, which eventually cost him three places in the standings.

A crash at Kansas the following week doomed any chance he had of winning the

Above: Edwards took a yellow-checkered win in the 2008 Auto Club 500 at Fontana.

Opposite: With a good start in 2005, Edwards goose-egged in 2006, but rebounded with three Cup wins in 2007 and added three more wins by mid-April 2008.

final Nextel Cup championship, and he finished ninth overall.

He did, though, win the final Busch Series championship, with back-to-back victories twice in the first half of the season, cruising home with a whopping 618-point margin over runner-up David Reutiman.

That was the culmination of a steady climb to the top in Busch: he was third and rookie of the year in 2005; second in 2006; first, and voted most popular driver, in 2007.

He also said he would compete in full schedules in both of NASCAR's top two — and re-branded — series in 2008, the Sprint Cup and Nationwide

"I just love to race," he said. "And I'm already at the track on Saturday sitting there in my motor coach with nothing else to do. They could race lawnmowers and I'd want to be in there."

All Edwards has ever wanted to do is race.

He grew up in Columbia, Missouri, the son of mid-western legend Carl Edwards Sr., who won more than 200 Modified and Midget races.

After taking rookie-of-the-year honors and a couple of track championships at Capital Speedway between 1998 and 2000, Edwards was ready to move up the ladder, but found no takers.

In 2001 he was still teaching school part time, living in his mother's basement, and racing without much success in the USAC Silver Crown Series.

Then he won the 2002 Baby Grand Stock Car Association national championship and earned seven Craftsman Truck rides for Mittler Brothers Motorsports. Roush soon recruited him for the 2003 Truck series. He responded by winning three races and the rookie-of-the-year title.

Roush had planned a steady climb for Edwards, but when Jeff Burton left for RCR in the middle of the 2004 season, Edwards was fast-forwarded directly to Cup racing.

Eyebrows were raised all around the paddock. But a month into his first full-time season in 2005, Edwards won both the Busch and Cup races at Atlanta, becoming the only driver to capture his first wins in two different series on the same weekend. His auspicious start propelled from virtual rags to immediate riches.

"I've never been middle class," Edwards laughs.

For the 2007 season, he moved back into the very Columbia house where he grew up, usually spending three days a week there, and getting away from the pressure and publicity of elite racing. His brother lives upstairs and his oldest friends are nearby.

"I just feel more like a normal person," he says, with a smile.

Edwards waits while his Roush Fenway Racing Ford gets fuel and tires in the 2008 Daytona 500. He finished 19th.

JEFF GORDON

It was, by all standards except one, a magnificent 2007 for Jeff Gordon. His wife, Ingrid Vandebosch, gave birth to daughter Emma, and Emma's dad won six Nextel Cup races, amassed by far the most points in the "regular season," roared past the Intimidator in career victories, was in first place halfway through the Chase, and set a NASCAR record with 30 top-10 finishes.

"It was an awesome year," Gordon conceded afterward. "But you know what? We wanted to win a championship and we got beat."

While he may have finished second, the season Gordon likes to call "the year that almost was" heralded his return to form.

In any other season, Gordon would have been Nextel Cup champ. He was second in the 2007 overall standings, finishing 77 points behind garage mate Johnson, the man he had mentored and brought to Hendrick Motorsports six years earlier. Gordon led the field by 317 points after 26 events, but when the standings were re-jigged for the 10-race Chase, he fell 20 points behind Johnson, who earned extra points for his six victories to Gordon's four.

By the middle of the Chase, Gordon was 68 points ahead again, after passing Johnson on a last-lap maneuver at Talladega, then winning the next week at Lowe's. But, like everyone else, he could only watch as Johnson reeled off four straight victories and his second

NO: 24

BORN:
August 4, 1971

HOMETOWN:
Vallejo, Calif.

TEAM:
Hendrick Motorsports

CAR: Chevrolet

SPONSOR: DuPont

CUP WINS: 81

CAREER EARNINGS:
$93,300,213

Previous page: Starting in Cup racing full time in 1993, Gordon has amassed more than $93 million in earnings, placed second in points in 2007.

Below: Under the eye of the NASCAR official (white helmet) at Bristol in 2008, Gordon's crew races to the driver side of the car to fit it with fresh tires. Gordon finished 11th.

straight championship, reminiscent of Gordon's brilliant 1998.

Only a few months earlier, Gordon seemed well past those salad days — the era when he refused to be beaten — when he won three championships in four years in the mid-1990s, when he added a fourth in 2001, when he and his Rainbow Warriors pit crew became the bunch every Dale Earnhardt fan loved to hate.

Gordon had finished 11th in the 2005 season, missing the Chase. When he was only sixth the following season, many observers thought his chances of challenging for a fifth title were done. But observers had been wrong about Gordon before, most notably in 1999 and 2000, when he finished sixth and ninth, respectively, and then won his fourth crown in 2001.

His latest rebound began in the midst of his worst campaign since his rookie year, when longtime crew chief Robbie Loomis gave way to 26-year-old Steve Letarte with 10 races left in the 2005 season. Gordon had three top-five finishes in the final five races and won at Martinsville in just his seventh race with Letarte.

They made it back to the Chase in 2006, with a pair of wins and 14 top-five finishes, and really cemented the recovery in 2007.

In April, Gordon won at Phoenix to tie the legendary Dale Earnhardt with 76 career wins, good for sixth all time. As pre-approved by Dale Earnhardt Jr. and his sister, Gordon took his victory lap holding a black, red and white flag with No. 3 emblazoned on it, as a tribute. But he was booed and pelted with beer cans by Earnhardt fans, as he was when he went past the legend the very next week at Talladega, with his 77th career win.

Gordon will never win over old-school racing fans, who have always been distrustful of his open-wheel roots, smooth style, corporate image and California upbringing.

Gordon's stepfather, John Bickford, bought him a Quarter Midget car when he was only four. Two years later he had won 35 main events and eventually won three national Quarter Midget titles and four national karting crowns. But he was running out of good competition, so his family moved to Pittsboro, Indiana, a state where racing — although open-wheel — was a religion and drivers were allowed to race at a younger age. By the time

he finished high school, he'd won more than 100 races.

After spending time at Buck Baker's driving school at North Carolina Speedway in 1990, he switched to stock cars and never looked back. Gordon's spent more years around stock car ovals than many of the people booing him.

Bill Davis Racing signed him to race the Busch Series in 1991, and he was named rookie of the year with a record 11 poles while also compiling three victories and an 11th-place overall finish. He also won the USAC Silver Crown series championship that summer.

Gordon moved full time into Winston Cup racing in 1993 and won rookie of the year, finishing eighth while winning the first Brickyard 400.

Soon he began one of the great four-year periods (1995–1998) in Cup racing history, accumulating 40 victories, winning three titles and coming up second to teammate Terry Labonte by only 37 points. In 1998 he tied two modern records, collecting four straight victories and 13 overall wins.

It took a season nearly as good as that one to beat Gordon in 2007.

Twice he won when his car limped across the finish line: first, spewing steam at Darlington in May, and then nearly out of gas at Lowe's in the midst of the Chase.

"If we were still racing under the old system, Jeff would be running away with it by now," Johnson said at the time. In the end, it was Gordon who had to pull alongside Johnson during his 2007 victory burnout to give his teammate's car a little bump and flash the thumbs-up sign.

"I thought this was our year to get another (title)," Gordon said. "But we're just coming up short at the crucial times."

Not that far short. But that's how high Gordon's standards are.

Budweiser Shootout action in 2008 saw four familiar drivers in close action at Daytona, especially Gordon, who is helping Stewart (20) down the track. Earnhardt (88) and Johnson (48) complete the quartet.

DENNY HAMLIN

NO: 11

BORN:
November 11, 1980

HOMETOWN:
Chesterfield, Va.

TEAM:
Joe Gibbs Racing

CAR: Toyota

SPONSOR: FedEX

CUP WINS: 3

CAREER EARNINGS:
$13,233,055

Denny Hamlin's stock has risen quickly and so has his temperature. Just four years after languishing at regional half-mile ovals and exhausting his financial backing, Hamlin finished among the top three drivers in the best stock car league in the world.

He followed up that rookie-of-the-year season by making the Chase again in 2007, but he also had two well-publicized verbal confrontations with other drivers.

Hamlin admits that he's moody and has "a short fuse" but also says he wants to learn to control of his emotions as well as he controls a race car.

In Hamlin's defence, the unanticipated success with which he burst onto the Cup scene created enormous pressures and expectations for his second season, which would strain even a hardened veteran.

The native of Chesterfield, Virginia, has always established himself in a hurry.

At the age of seven, he won the first go-kart race he entered. At 16 he switched to stock cars, and in his debut at Langley Speedway, took the pole, set a new track record and won the race.

At 25, he warmed up for his first full-time Cup season by winning the Budweiser Shootout. It was the first shootout win ever by a rookie and foreshadowed Hamlin's spectacular 2006.

He swept both Pocono events after taking the pole each time, had six other top-five

results, became the first true rookie to qualify for the Chase, and finished third overall, the second-best standing by a rookie in Cup annals.

In 2007 he won the third race of his brief career, bobbling a bit in the stretch at a July race in New Hampshire, but holding off hard-charging Jeff Gordon by .068 seconds.

That victory was his 10th top-10 finish in 13 races, which eventually propelled him into the Chase. But in the playoff itself, he had only three results better than 15th, and finished a distant 12th among the 12 qualifiers.

"I don't know if I would call it a sophomore slump, because we made the Chase and we ran strong all year," Hamlin said. "It seems like when Chase time came around we had tough luck, and that's something I didn't have last year. It kind of plagued us at the wrong time."

He was also plagued by two high-profile incidents. At the Pepsi 400 in Daytona, with Hamlin and Joe Gibbs Racing teammate Tony Stewart running one–two, they crashed and wrecked both cars. Stewart, quick to blame, confronted him angrily and Joe Gibbs himself had to fly south to mediate the dispute.

At Dover in September, Hamlin collided with the rear of Kyle Petty's car. Petty went to Hamlin's garage stall, leaned into the cockpit, shook his finger and slapped Hamlin's visor down. Hamlin quickly crawled out the window to chase Petty, but crew members intervened.

Above: Hamlin's FedEx sponsored Toyota is quite somber compared to the brightly-colored Camry of Kyle Busch, both seen here during the Gatorade Duels 150 at Daytona in February 2008.

Opposite: It's taken only four years for Hamlin to go from the bullrings of his native Virginia to the pinnacle of stock car racing.

Hamlin later apologized for his response and was clearly contrite. And he was brutally honest — informative — in his self-examination.

"It's hard for the fan to understand who I am," he told reporters. "I didn't get here because of my last name. I didn't get here because we had money. I'm trying my best to portray a good image, but I'm trying my best to be myself, all in the same breath. It's tough to have a personality and show it to everyone without being criticized. Right now, I'm just trying to find that balance."

Hamlin's parents, Dennis and Mary Lou, owned and financed their son's cars as he won various track championships at Langley and Southside Speedways in Virginia, and started having success in late models at Southampton Motor Speedway.

But, after taking out mortgages on their house and selling two classic cars, they were out of money in late 2002. As Hamlin stood in a registration line for what he figured was his final race before returning to work

at his father's trailer-hitch business, he was approached by Jim Dean, a car owner who had heard of his financial plight.

Dean offered to pay for his next race, and soon offered him a ride for 2003. Hamlin responded by winning a whopping 25 of 36 starts and the championship at Southern National Speedway.

Meanwhile, Dean began supplying cars for JGR's diversity program, and when Hamlin surpassed track records while merely setting the cars up, an impressed J.D. Gibbs offered him a developmental contract for 2004.

Hamlin repaid Gibbs' faith with five Craftsmen Trucks races in 2004 and one Busch race, an eighth place at Darlington.

In 2005 he was fifth in the Busch Series standings, and beat out J.J. Yeley for the vacant No. 11 Cup car, finishing with three top-10s in seven late-season races. And in 2006 he shot directly into the upper tier of Cup racing.

Just two years after JGR's company president took a flyer on a young driver with very little national experience, Hamlin had become a contender for the Cup championship.

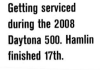

Getting serviced during the 2008 Daytona 500. Hamlin finished 17th.

KEVIN HARVICK

You win the biggest race of the season in one of the most frantic finishes ever, you qualify for the Chase, your truck wins the series championship, and you're still plagued by discontent.

You must be Kevin Harvick.

"If somebody had told us at the beginning of the season that we would win the 500, the All-Star race and make the Chase, we would have been pretty happy," Harvick said after the 2007 season. "However, since we are such competitors, we have been pretty disappointed this year when things didn't go our way."

Harvick had set the bar pretty high for himself in 2006 when he won five races in his sixth Cup season, which is as many races as he had won

in his first five years combined. So when he captured a wild Daytona 500 to open the following year, he was understandably expecting a lot more than a 10th place overall finish.

But two consecutive appearances in the Chase marked the most consistent back-to-back seasons of Harvick's mercurial Cup career, which began in 2001 when his carefully planned progression was unexpectedly accelerated by the death of legend Dale Earnhardt.

Six years to the day after the Intimidator was killed after hitting the wall on the perilous turn four in the Daytona 500, Harvick audaciously bolted past sentimental favorite Mark Martin high on the same turn and held on to win a furious drag race by .02 seconds.

NO: 29
BORN:
December 8, 1975
HOMETOWN:
Bakersfield, Calif.
TEAM:
Richard Childress Racing
CAR: Chevrolet
SPONSOR:
Shell-Penzoil
CUP WINS: 11
CAREER EARNINGS:
$42,432,766

Harvick leads a small group in the 2008 Food City 500 at Bristol. He finished second behind Jeff Burton

Behind the two neck-and-neck leaders there were crashes galore, and Martin may have hesitated a split second thinking a caution flag would be raised. But officials ruled that the yellow didn't come up until Harvick had taken the lead.

Still, NASCAR had to review the tape to determine the winner of a wild race, which ended well after dusk.

"I knew we had won and I got so excited I punched the dang mirror out of the car," said Harvick, who's never been known for masking his feelings. "My go-kart experience paid off because I didn't let off the floor and and we just kept bouncing off everything. This is the Daytona 500! Can you believe it?"

Harvick had a solid 2007, qualifying for the Chase, winning six Busch races, and sharing ownership of Ron Hornaday's Mastercraft Series-winning truck with his wife, DeLana Harvick.

That didn't compare, though, to 2006, when he won five Cup races, finished fourth overall, tied for the most top-five finishes with 15 and made a mockery of the Busch Series, clinching the title with a month of racing left.

Harvick began racing karts while still in kindergarten and over the next 10 years won seven national titles and two Grand National championships. After various class titles at his home track in Bakersfield and NASCAR's Southwest Series and West Series, plus

Previous page: Harvick's biggest highlight so far has been winning the 2007 Daytona 500. He also has numerous Busch series wins to his credit, and a Craftsman Truck title.

11 top-10 finishes in the 1999 Craftsman Truck Series, Harvick was hired by Childress for the 2000 Busch Series.

He won three times, was named rookie of the year and the following season was unexpectedly at the wheel for 35 Cup races. He was named Cup rookie of the year, and added the Busch championship, becoming the only driver to accomplish that double.

After his fine rookie season, he plunged from ninth to 21st overall in 2002, but he rebounded to place fifth in 2003.

Harvick then slumped to a pair of 14th-place finishes as all Childress cars struggled with their engines, prompting organizational changes. Harvick also struggled with other drivers, engaging in some heated verbal jousts.

RCR got its act together for 2006 and so did Harvick, with what he called the single best season of his career. He couldn't replicate it in 2007 but did reap two of the richest harvests of the season: $1.5 million for the Daytona win; $1 million for the non-points All Star Classic at Lowe's.

And in characteristic Harvick style, he challenged himself and RCR to get better in the future: "I think we just have to just elevate the performance on everything."

Harvick in his Richard Childress Racing Chevrolet, shown here in a 2008 Bristol pit stop.

JIMMIE JOHNSON

NO: 48

BORN:
September 17, 1975

HOMETOWN:
El Cajon, Calif.

TEAM:
Hendrick
Motorsports

CAR: Chevrolet

SPONSOR: Lowe's

CUP WINS: 33

CAREER EARNINGS:
$59,531,336

For most athletes, momentum is a friend. For Jimmie Johnson, it's a blood brother.

When the quiet Californian gets on a roll he's difficult, if not impossible, to stop. You've got to pin him down in his dog days of summer because his Big Dog days come in autumn.

Johnson won both the 2006 and 2007 Cup points titles with an aggressive driving style that produced consistently brilliant climaxes. After finishing in the top five in his first four major league years, including a pair of runner-up seasons, Johnson became series winner in 2006 by recording a victory and four second-place finishes over the last six races of the Chase.

As spectacular as that run to the wire was, he drove right past it in 2007 by assertively winning Chase races Nos. 6, 7, 8 and 9 before finishing a cautious seventh in the finale to clinch his second straight title.

Over the 10 races that made up the second half of the Chase in those two seasons, Johnson had five wins, three seconds, a seventh and a ninth.

No one ever doubted that Johnson was going to win championships, least of all his close friend Jeff Gordon, who had talked Rick Hendrick into signing Johnson seven years earlier, and is also co-owner of the No. 48 Chevy.

Like Gordon, Johnson is a Californian who says the right things, inspires respect but not

passion, and is rarely surrounded by controversy. And like Gordon, he can turn on the pressure when it counts.

It was Gordon whom Johnson caught and passed for the 2007 championships, and his back-to-back titles were the first since Gordon did it in 1997–98.

Johnson became the 10th driver to win two straight championships and, with 10 race victories, was the first to reach double figures since Gordon had 13 in 1998. "I'm lucky to be in cars that can win races, and have a pit crew that can put me in that position," Johnson says modestly.

In the 2007 Chase event at Texas, Johnson and Matt Kenseth were going door-to-door

over the final seven laps. Hendrick was tempted to ask Knaus to have Johnson play it safe, finish second, and not chance a wreck that would squander important points. But Knaus never even thought of backing off because he and Johnson wanted to compete hard, not just "points race." Johnson won the wild showdown, for his third consecutive victory, and pulled a decisive 30 points ahead of Gordon.

The year before, Johnson was in seventh place, trailing leader Jeff Burton by 146 points halfway through the Chase. But by the season finale, he needed only a safe ninth place finish to comfortably beat runner-up Matt Kenseth for his first title.

Above: During Budweiser Shootout practice, Johnson (48) got turned around in a melee with Jeff Gordon (24), David Gilliand (38) and Bill Elliott (21).

Opposite: This quiet Californian lets his car do the talking for him, and together they have mastered the language of NASCAR.

His 2006 ending was indicative of his career pattern. In 2005 he led the points race for 16 weeks but had three races outside the top 25 in August and early September. In 2004 he won eight times, but scuffled through four races in August and eventually lost the closest title run in Cup history to Kurt Busch by eight points. He foreshadowed what was to come, though, by winning four times and finishing second once, in 2004's final six races.

"I don't know why the cycle goes like it does," Johnson said in 2007, after he'd had back-to-back finishes of 37th and 39th in July. "We tried to address what to do in the summer but didn't have the results."

He started as a motocrosser at age five, and by the time he was 15 Johnson was the youngest driver ever to compete in the Mickey Thompson Stadium Truck Series. He won three Thompson titles, won three other major off-road championships from 1994 to 1997, and then switched to stock cars, winning 1997 rookie of the year in the ASA Challenge Series.

He got into five Busch Series races in 1999, and in 2001 finished eighth overall driving for Herzog Motorsports.

After an unspectacular trial for Hendrick in three Winston Cup races in late 2001, Johnson won the pole at the 2002 Daytona 500 — just the third rookie to do so.

Four years later, he won the Daytona 500 and also took the checkered flag at the Brickyard 400, joining Dale Jarrett as the only other driver to triumph at the continent's two most famous tracks in the same season.

"Finishing second in 2004 and 2005 taught us a lot, although it was painful," Johnson said. "And it's led to these two championships. I feel that you can try too hard, and I've tried too hard in the past to win races, and even to win championships. It's more a clear picture now."

So clear that his owner envisions more of the same.

"I don't see anything that's going to slow Jimmie down," said Rick Hendrick. "We can do some phenomenal things in the future."

They're already doing some phenomenal things in the present.

Johnson ahead of eventual 2008 Food City 500 winner Kyle Busch at Bristol. He finished 18th despite starting on the pole.

KASEY KAHNE

Kasey Kahne helped lead the recent invasion by precocious drivers known by NASCAR fans as the "Young Guns." But in 2007 his aim was off and he was consistently outdrawn.

Nobody welcomed the infusion of George Gillett capital into Evernham Motorsports more than the 2004 rookie of the year. His production plummeted so severely in 2007 that it was clear that the brilliant Ray Evernham needed to spend as much time as he could around the garage, rather than working on the financial side of the business.

"It wasn't just one thing," Kahne understated. "It was everything."

Every little thing. Every big thing. From the

company's inability to afford the best testing apparatus, to equipment failure, to a tumble from a stunning six wins in 2006 to a stunned zero in 2007, the season was essentially a write-off for the enormously popular Kahne.

But he emerged from the 2007 darkness with a major coup: he was chosen as Budweiser's NASCAR face when brewing giant shifted sponsorship from Dale Earnhardt Jr. to the No. 9 Dodge.

Kahne himself had noted that he hasn't enjoyed as much success in the odd-numbered seasons as he has in the even-numbered ones, dating back to the days before he burst onto the Cup scene.

Indeed, after he finished 13th, won four poles

NO: **9**

BORN: **April 10, 1980**

HOMETOWN: **Enumclaw, Wash.**

TEAM: **Gillett Evernham Motorsports**

CAR: **Dodge**

SPONSOR: **Budweiser**

CUP WINS: **7**

CAREER EARNINGS: **$24,110,117**

Previous page: One of the sport's young guns, Kahne picked up six Cup wins in 2006, but stumbled in 2007.

and was top rookie in 2004, he endured the Cup series' traditional sophomore slump and dropped all the way to 23rd in 2005.

But even the questionable on-again, off-again theory doesn't cast a full light on just how far Kahne plummetted in 2007.

Kahne had finished eighth overall in 2006, but led all Cup drivers with six wins and six poles The next year, as the team just couldn't get either the standard car or Car of Tomorrow model set up properly, he didn't win at all, but had only one top-five finish all season and stumbled through a joyless 16-week stretch in which he didn't record a single top-10 result.

Worse, he slid from a series-leading 706 fastest-laps-run to just 183 in 2007. His decline in Driver Rating from 94.3 in 2006 to 71.5 the next season was the most severe on the circuit.

And as he entered the 2008 season he was facing charges, and a civil suit, over a run-in with a security guard at Homestead on the final weekend of the season.

Below: Kahne and his Dodge in the pits during the UAW-Dodge 400 at Las Vegas in 2008. He came from 37th to place sixth.

Things could only look up for Kahne and he was taking solace from a second-place finish at Bristol — Evernham's only top-five result of the year — and six consecutive top-20 finishes during the Chase.

"Last year we had it figured out, and this year we haven't," Kahne mused as he tried to put 2007 well behind him.

Kasey Kahne leads a small pack of Cup drivers coming into the pits in the Goody's Cool Orange 500 at Martinsville. Kahne placed 17th in the Gillett/Evernham Motorsports Dodge.

Kahne has been behind a wheel since his father built him a banked eighth-of-a-mile oval on the family farm in Enumclaw, Washington. He began racing his friends in four-wheelers on that track when he was eight years old.

Moving to the dirt ovals scattered around his home state, Kahne quickly showed promise and at 16 won 11 of 14 races, the Northwest Mini-Sprint Car title and the track championship at Hannigan Speedway. Two years later he won 12 full-sized Sprint Car races.

In 2000 he was signed by legendary car owner Steve Lewis to run USAC schedules in Sprint, Midget and Silver Crown Series. He won the Midget championship and was rookie of the year in the Silver Bullet Series. The following year he ran a partial schedule in the Toyota Atlantic Series and the Formula Ford 2000 Series before deciding to make a full-time switch to stock cars.

Kahne signed to race in the Busch Series with Robert Yates Racing in 2002 and with Akins Motorsports the following season. As a rookie he was seventh overall and in 2003 won the final Busch race of the season, at Homestead, for his first NASCAR national series victory.

With Bill Elliott easing into semi-retirement, Evernham signed Kahne for the 2004 season. After an undistinguished 41st at the Daytona 500 he had two seconds and a third, to become just the seventh driver to record three top-fives in his first four Cup starts. He ended the season in exactly the same way, with three top-fives in the final four races, to give him 13 for the year, and rookie-of-the-year honors. He missed the Chase by a paltry 28 points before dropping off to 13th overall.

Kahne plunged to 23rd in the 2005 points championship, maybe because it was an odd-number year, but largely because nine times his car could not finish a race, representing a full quarter of the schedule.

He did, however, come out of the down year with his first Cup victory, out-duelling Tony Stewart at Richmond in May. His debut trip to Victory Lane came in his 47th start, after he had been runner-up six times.

"The best thing about it is that I don't have to answer 'When are you going to win?' anymore," he said at the time.

The question people ask now is, when will Khane win again?

MATT KENSETH

NO: 17

BORN: March 10, 1972

HOMETOWN: Cambridge, Wisc.

TEAM: Roush Fenway Racing

CAR: Ford

SPONSOR: DeWALT

CUP WINS: 16

CAREER EARNINGS: $51,726,470

If consistency had a face, it would look exactly like Matt Kenseth.

When it comes to top-10 finishes, the 2003 Winston Cup champion is as steady as a metronome.

Since 2002 he has ended among the top-10 drivers every season, a streak matched in that period by only Jimmie Johnson. In those six years Kenseth racked up 15 wins and averaged exactly 20 top-10 finishes per season. And in a three-year stretch from 2005–07 he came home from an astonishing 40 races with top-five results.

Had it not been for a four-race collapse early in the 2007 Chase, when crashes and engine failures relegated him to 35th twice, 34th and 26th, Kenseth might have been in the hunt for his second career title.

As it was, he finished fourth overall, notching a victory in the last race of the Nextel Cup era, and the last with veteran Robbie Reiser as his crew chief. Reiser moved up to vice-president of Roush-Fenway Racing and Chip Bolin, who's worked with Kenseth's team since it began, graduated to crew chief.

"The thing I'm most fired up about is I see the company going in the right direction," the even-keeled Kenseth said. "And I feel like we're gaining momentum."

They already had a lot of momentum. Kenseth has always been able to muster up long stretches of upper-echelon driving, as

indicated by his top-five finishes in each of the last five 2007 Chase races. And for 23 of the 26 weeks of the "regular season," he was among the top-five in the points standings.

In 2006 he won four times, including the second back-to-back sweep (Michigan and Bristol) of his career, dropping off the top-10 leader board just once on the way to finishing second overall to Johnson.

In 2005 Kenseth blew an engine in the Daytona 500 to open the season in 42nd place, the first time he'd been out of the Cup's top 10 in 71 weeks, and by the mid-point of the racing calendar he had only a single top-five result. But over the final 19 events of the season, he harvested a victory and 10 other

top-10 finishes to climb to seventh overall.

Kenseth has risen steadily and surely into the aristocracy of stock car racing after earning his spurs on the demanding short tracks of his native Wisconsin.

In 1991, when he was 19, he became the youngest driver to win a feature in the ARTGO Challenge Series. (The former record was held by Mark Martin, who would eventually become his garage mate at Roush Racing.)

In 1995 Kenseth won track titles at both Madison International Speedway and Wisconsin International Raceway.

In 1997 he stood in second place in the American Speed Association when Reiser got him behind the wheel for 21 Busch Series

Above: Kenseth runs ahead of Brian Vickers at Martinsville in 2008, where he wound up 30th.

Opposite: Called "Mr. Consistency" by some, Kenseth, who has been behind the wheel of a Cup car since 2000, won the championship in 2003.

races. Despite that partial schedule, he finished second in the Busch rookie standings. The next year he won three Busch races, finished second to Dale Earnhardt Jr. in the series points race and got his first Cup start, finishing a remarkable sixth at Dover, as Bill Elliott's sub.

Jack Roush gave Kenseth a full-time Cup ride in 2000, and reaped immediate dividends. Kenseth became the first freshman to win the Coca-Cola 600, was named rookie of the year and finished in the top-10 in nearly one-third (11) of his starts.

He slumped slightly in 2001 and didn't win a race, it was the last season he was blanked. But he won a series-high five times in 2002, finishing eighth overall, and rode that wave all the way to the 2003 championship.

His title, the last of the Winston Cup era, was built on a career-high 25 finishes in the top-10, an admirable consistency. But he won only once all year, which accelerated the call for change and paved the way for the playoff concept of the Chase.

Kenseth's 2007 wasn't that far off his championship form of 2003. He had one more win and two more top-fives than he did in his title year and just three fewer top 10's. Over the final five races of the Chase he rocketed from 12th to fourth overall.

Jimmie Johnson captured the first four of those final five races, while Kenseth dominated the season finale for his first career win at Homestead. That clear victory gave his team optimism for 2008 and '09, and a wistful look at what might have been in 2007.

"Obviously there were a couple bad weeks in there, but I think our performance in the Chase without the problems was good enough to win any other Chase besides this one," Kenseth said, in reference to the 2007 domination of Johnson and Jeff Gordon.

Roush-Fenway didn't have the success some other shops did in those early 2007 CoT races. But by the latter part of the season they had made up the lost ground. And Kenseth was delivering in the car that is now the Cup's standard model.

Nobody expected anything different.

A native of Wisconsin, Kenseth, seen here at a 2008 Daytona 500 pitstop, ran the ARTGO and ASA tours before heading south.

RYAN NEWMAN

When your nickname is Rocket Man, it's pretty noticeable when you begin to fly a lot closer to ground.

Ryan Newman, who pole-vaulted his way to NASCAR fame by qualifying first in a stunning number of Cup races, endured a massive slump in 2006.

And even though a solid rebound in 2007 fueled Newman's legion of fans with justifiable reason for optimism, Newman was bothered by some troubling statistics.

In his first four full seasons of Cup racing, from 2002–05, Newman won 12 races, inherited his nickname by winning 34 poles and never finished out of the top 10 in the points race.

Over the next two years, Newman failed to win a race, sat on only nine poles, had just nine top-5 results and finished 18th and 13th, respectively, in the points race.

The good news was that 2007 was a huge improvement over 2006, which might eventually be viewed as one of those off-years that almost every NASCAR driver seems to face during his career.

In finishing 13th, best among non-contenders for the Chase, Newman was taken out of the running by circumstances beyond his control in one-quarter of the 2007 events. He was caught up in accidents in four races and had engine problems in another five. And, he probably would have won at Lowe's Speedway

NO: 12

BORN:
December 8, 1977

HOMETOWN:
South Bend, Ind.

TEAM: Penske Racing

CAR: Dodge

SPONSOR: Alltel

CUP WINS: 12

CAREER EARNINGS:
$37,340,232

during the Chase, when he took the pole and had the lead on a late restart, if he hadn't crashed due to a tire problem and sagged to 28th.

That was one of the few detours in an impressive finishing flourish that gave him three top-5 finishes in the final five races of the 2007 season. And he returned to his familiar spot on the starting grid, with five poles, second to series leader Jeff Gordon's seven.

Still, he missed the Chase for the second straight season, after finishing no lower than seventh overall in his first four Cup seasons.

Newman had been struggling at the tail end of his successful streak, as most Dodge drivers battled with aerodynamic problems in 2005. That might have precipitated his steep decline in 2006.

He has been accused of driving a bit too conservatively on Sunday, after going for broke in Friday pole qualifying, but his Cup-high

eight wins in 2003 demonstrated that he is certainly able to deliver the goods when it counts most.

Newman grew up in Indiana, the heart of open-wheel country, but says he "always wanted to race stock cars."

He started in Quarter Midget competition when he was five and later became a superstar in Midget cars. At 15, he was rookie of the year and series champion in the All-American Midget Series. In ensuing years he also took top rookie honors in USAC National Midgets, USAC Silver Crown and Sprint Cars.

A Silver Crown national title in 1999 gave him an ARCA ride in 2000, and when he took three checkered flags that season, Roger Penske offered him a Cup start at Phoenix.

Through all of this racing, Newman was attending Purdue University, studying vehicle structural engineering.

"My dad always said that you're going to get

your education before you go full-time racing," Newman explained. "Roger Penske wanted me to have my diploma before we started racing. That makes a big difference."

When he graduated in the summer of 2001 he became one of the rare Cup racers to have earned a university degree.

"I wish that more drivers had an education," he said. "People don't want to wait for kids to be out of college to hire them to be a race car driver."

With Newman's education complete, Penske provided him with seven more Cup rides in 2001, and he finished two of them in the top five. Meanwhile he also competed in two ARCA races and 15 Busch Series events, winning at Michigan and grabbing six poles.

That year, in just his third career Cup start, Newman tied Mark Martin's record for earliest pole in a career, laying the foundation of his Rocket Man reputation.

In 2002 Newman broke through to elite Cup status, capturing his first victory, at New Hampshire. He won a tight battle with Jimmie Johnson for the rookie-of-the-year title, led

the series with 22 top-10 finishes, tying a rookie record, and also set a new first-year mark by winning six poles.

He finished sixth overall, a spot he would occupy again in 2003 and 2005, slipping only slightly to seventh in 2004. And he won the Bud Light Pole Award (most starts in the No.1 position) four seasons in a row.

Then came the downturn of 2006, and the relative upswing of 2007. His 10-point improvement in NASCAR's Driver Rating was the largest of all non-contenders for the Chase, but he'll need that much again to get back into the very top tier.

The 2008 season opened with Roy McCauley as Newman's crew chief, succeeding Mike Nelson, who was promoted to Penske's vice-president of operations. McCauley and Newman combined to claim six victories in just nine Busch Series races in 2005 and they indicated they were ready to get back to Newman's earlier form with a win at the 2008 Daytona 500.

The Newman victory party after winning the 2008 Daytona 500. The former Midget, Sprint Car, and Silver Crown driver from Indiana has made the big time.

TONY STEWART

NO: 20

BORN: May 20, 1971

HOMETOWN:
Columbus, Ind.

TEAM:
Joe Gibbs Racing

CAR: Toyota

SPONSOR:
Home Depot

CUP WINS: 32

CAREER EARNINGS:
$65,240,202

Tony Stewart doesn't always win the driver's championship, but the road to it usually goes right through him.

The outspoken former open-wheeler captured the 2005 Nextel Cup championship and the 2002 Winston Cup title, and as the Sprint Cup era opens, he's not likely to be far from the centre of things. On or off the track.

Controversy does seem to find Stewart, but he doesn't hide from it either.

After his team owner, Joe Gibbs, summoned him for a very direct talk between the 2004 and 2005 seasons, and told him his frequent angry outbursts were affecting the whole garage, Stewart displayed a kinder, gentler demeanor. Except behind the wheel.

And Team Happy reveled in that 2005 championship together, whereas the 2002 winning campaign was "torture" for everyone, Stewart recalls.

But Stewart still likes to blow up at the media and take verbal shots at other drivers. However, he can sprinkle in just enough dollops of charm to keep everyone off-balance. And he usually makes it tough for others out on the pavement, especially after he's gone through a little adversity.

After he finished 18th in his backup car at Richmond, the last qualifying race for the 2006 Chase, and missed the 10-driver playoff by a mere 16 points, Stewart played spoiler the rest of the way home. He won three Chase

races and was runner-up in a fourth, directly influencing the final standings.

In 2007 he had a very public spat with teammate Denny Hamlin after a collision when they were running 1–2 in the Pepsi 400, and Stewart ended up in 38th place. Gibbs again flew into town to smooth things over and Stewart went on to win three of the next four races and break the longest victory drought (22 races) of his Cup career.

"I'm glad to have the monkey off our backs," he shrugged. "But I wasn't freaking out about it."

His three victories, while finishing sixth overall, in 2007 were two fewer than he had in 2006 when he finished 11th, the worst placing of his eight-year Cup career, but his timing was better. He entered the 2007 Chase in third place, but had only two top-five finishes in the playoff run.

After two drivers outside the Chase, Paul Menard and Kasey Kahne, collided with his car in pit row during the fifth race of the Chase, knocking him down several positions, Stewart complained that drivers eliminated from the points race can affect those who are still vying for the title. Of course, as an eliminated driver, his three Chase wins in 2006 certainly affected those still in it.

After a frustrating race early in the 2007 season, Stewart hinted at retirement when his contract with Gibbs runs out after the 2009 season.

Above: A new paint scheme for a new car in 2008. Stewart is the number one driver in the Joe Gibbs Racing stable, and the Chevrolets have been dropped for Toyotas.

Opposite: Tony Stewart is one of the sport's most colorful racers as he is known for criticizing other drivers. His two championship titles give him a little leeway in this regard.

"We'll assess where we're at and whether we're still having fun or not," he said. "If we are, we'll stay. If we're not we'll go do something else. I made my father a promise when I was a kid, that the day I wasn't having fun driving race cars any more, I'd quit. It's not exactly the safest sport to just participate in if you're not having a good time doing it."

Stewart's father, Nelson, owned the karts and was his crew chief when he was growing up an hour south of Indianapolis Motor Speedway. As a boy, Stewart fantasized about winning a race at the famous track.

By the time he was 12, he had won an International Karting Federation championship, and four years later he was World Karting Association national champion.

After winning the USAC National Midget title in 1994, and becoming the first driver to sweep the USAC Triple Crown — National Midget, Spring and Silver Crown — in 1995, he broke into the IRL. He was rookie of the year in 1996 and series champion the following season.

In the midst of that open-wheel success, he also flirted with NASCAR, competing in nine Busch Series races for Ranier/Walsh Racing in 1996.

Gibbs vowed he'd land him for NASCAR, and Stewart ran 27 Busch races for the popular owner and NFL coach through 1997 and 1998, winning three times and taking '98 rookie of the year honors.

Stewart graduated full time to Winston Cup in 1999, winning three races, finishing fourth overall and earning another rookie of the year title. He was runner-up to Jeff Gordon in 2001 and in 2002, took his first Cup title, by 31 points over Mark Martin.

Martin was among those who spoke to Stewart that season, advising him to stop letting small annoyances get in the way of larger accomplishments.

For the most part, he listened and in his second title year of 2005, there were no dramatic scenes when he fell to 10th in mid-June of what he thought then was "the worst season of we'd ever had."

He rallied from that low point to win the title, and along the way started the fence-climbing routine that has become part of his post-victory repertoire.

He also won the Brickyard 400, his first win in 15 attempts in three different series at the track that made his home state famous. If he died the next day, he said, he would die happy.

It was an emotional statement, but in Tony Stewart's world there is a lot of emotion.

"Smoke," as Stewart is known, does have his moments. Here he is spinning in the 2008 Food City 500 at Bristol. He finished 14th after starting sixth.

MARTIN TRUEX JR.

Now that he's not living in a shadow, Martin Truex Jr. wants to cast one.

"It's always been me going to someone for help," Truex Jr. said as he geared up for the 2008 Sprint Cup season. "I think we've got to the point now where we can start doing some great things for the company, helping the younger drivers out."

After the terse announcement that Dale Earnhardt, Inc. would lose the founders' son, and senior driver, Dale Jr., to Hendrick Motorsports at the end of the 2007 season, "the other Junior" attracted a tidal wave of attention.

Truex Jr. was losing his mentor and close friend, the shepherd who had brought him to NASCAR's national events, first for two

spectacular Busch Series seasons driving for Chance 2, then for a full-time ride in the Show, piloting DEI's long-idle No. 1 car.

It was early in his second full Cup season that Truex Jr. found out that Earnhardt was heading to Hendrick. He was saddened, but also saw the opportunity and in the weeks following the official announcement, jumped from 20th to 10th in the points standings. He qualified for his first Chase in seventh place, finishing 11th overall, five spots ahead of Earnhardt.

He also won his first Cup race, in his 58th start, at Dover as part of a dominant five-week early summer stretch in which he had four top-three finishes.

NO: 1
BORN: **June 29, 1980**
HOMETOWN:
Mayetta, N.J.
TEAM:
Dale Earnhardt, Inc.
CAR: **Chevrolet**
SPONSOR:
Bass Pro Shops
CUP WINS: 1
CAREER EARNINGS:
$11,767,975

Previous page: Truex will be waving the flag at DEI now that Dale Jr. is gone. The former Busch Series star could be on his way to big things if given the opportunity.

Below: Truex Jr. pits during the Kobalt Tools 500 at the Atlanta Motor Speedway in 2008. He started the race third and finished 21st.

"I took it as an insult every time I read that we were going to suck now that Junior was leaving," Truex Jr. said at the time.

Although he completed the 2007 Chase strongly, with top 10s in the last three races, Truex Jr.'s struggles through September and October took him out of the hunt for the title.

"It seemed like we couldn't go one week without having a pit-road incident or a flat tire or bad luck or something on the race track or blowing motors," he said.

The horizon may be considerably brighter for Truex Jr. In separate mid-season agreements in 2007, DEI arranged to build and develop engines with Richard Childress Racing and bring veteran Mark Martin's savvy into the stable via a merger with Ginn Racing.

And it may not be too long before Truex Jr. can top the standings in Sprint Cup racing, as he did for his only two full seasons in the Busch Series.

Racing for Chance 2, the Busch team owned by Earnhardt Jr. and his stepmother Teresa, Truex Jr. won the 2004 series title in a season-

long battle with Kyle Busch. He won four of the first 12 races, and six overall, to become the first rookie to win the Busch Series title since Dale Jr. won in 1998.

Early in the next season, he was in eighth place 400 points back of the top spot, but rallied to win six races, including NASCAR's first incursion into Mexico, and beat Clint Bowyer by 69 points for the title.

"There was no in-between," Truex Jr. said of becoming the first back-to-back Busch winner since Earnhardt Jr. six years earlier. "We were either great or terrible."

His Busch Series results made Truex Jr. one of the hottest commodities on the market, with Penske South and Roush Racing both rumored to be interested in his services. DEI wisely signed him to a three-year deal.

The New Jersey native had first come to DEI's attention during a four-year stretch driving a family-owned car in the Busch North Series. His father Martin Sr. was a well-known fixture in Modified and Busch North races in the northeast, and won a major Busch North race at New Hampshire in 1994. He also raced

a few times on the Busch Series, with a 12th place finish at Nazareth in 1994.

But in 2000, Truex Sr. unselfishly stepped out of his car so his son could race it in the Busch North Series. Later that season, 20-year-old Truex Jr. won his first series race at, appropriately, New Hampshire setting a track record and leading flag to flag against a far more experienced field.

Truex Jr. continued to win and set Busch North track records through 2003, but meanwhile caught the attention of DEI vice-president Richie Gilmore, who is from the area. Gilmour tipped Earnhardt Jr., who gave Truex some part-time work in his Busch Series car.

He had three top-10s in six races, and the next year had a full time ride.

In 2005, when Dale Jr. was injured, Truex Jr. qualfied his Cup for him at … where else? … New Hampshire, and the following season he was behind the wheel of the No. 1 car. He finished third in the rookie standings and 17th overall, but had a second-place finish in the season's last race at Homestead.

Now he is in the lead role on a team founded by a legend, and like the Jr. who led DEI before him, the pressure to win is treated as just one of the perks of the job. If Truex Jr. fills in for Dale Jr. the way he has his entire career, DEI will be just fine.

Truex at speed during practice at the Kobalt Tools 500 at Atlanta, 2008. The New Jersey native will have new teammate Mark Martin as his mentor with the DEI organization.

Brian Vickers at speed in his Red Bull Toyota
at Texas Motor Speedway, April 2008.

PATRICK CARPENTIER

NO: 10

BORN:
August 13, 1971

HOMETOWN:
Joliette, Quebec,
Canada

TEAM:
Gillett Evernham
Motorsports

CAR: Dodge

SPONSOR: Valvoline

CUP WINS: 0

CAREER EARNINGS:
$214,800

When Patrick Carpentier was growing up in Quebec every kid playing street hockey wore the No. 10 sweater of Montreal Canadiens superstar Guy Lafleur.

Decades later, at center ice before an NHL game in Montreal, Lafleur presented Carpentier with his own No. 10 sweater, to commemorate the open-wheel driver's jump to Sprint Cup racing in the No. 10 car.

Such symbolism seems to fit Carpentier, who exemplifies NASCAR's gravitational pull on a passel of open-wheel drivers and international stars.

It was only a few days after purchasing a majority interest in Evernham Motors that Canadiens' owner, George Gillett, announced the signing of the fan-and-sponsor-friendly Carpentier.

The company had been impressed with Carpentier's performance in the inaugural Busch Series race in Montreal in July 2007, when he drove a Fritz Motorsports car to the pole and a second-place finish. That earned him a second Busch start, this time for Evernham Motors, at Watkins Glen. A day later, he made his first Cup start in the No. 10 Dodge, led seven laps, and finished 22nd, up 18 from his starting slot.

Carpentier replaced Scott Riggs for the final two races of the 2007 season, qualifying but finishing only 33rd and 40th.

Carpentier remained optimistic, however, as his career had taken a sudden upswing, making him one of the fastest-rising drivers in the sport. For the better part of two seasons before he signed with Gillett Evernham, his career had reached an impasse. He had grown disenchanted with the IRL, where he still had opportunities for rides but wasn't making much progress in his goal of reaching the Sprint Cup circuit.

It's been a long and winding road, literally, for Carpentier to reach the banked ovals of NASCAR.

He began racing go-karts at the comparatively advanced age of 13, but learned quickly and won the Canadian 4-stroke title the next season

In 1987 he earned a three-day course at Spenard/Davis racing school by working as a mechanic, and won the school's Formula Ford 2000 runoffs. Two years later, he won the school Formula Ford 2000 championship, leading to a limited schedule on the Canadian Formua l Ford 2000 circuit.

In 1992 he captured the Canadian Players Atlantic Championship and in 1996, his second full-time year in the Toyota Atlantic Series, he captured the championship, by winning nine times in 12 races.

That tied the record established by Quebec-born icon Gilles Villeneuve. In his early years on the track, Carpentier had often raced against Gilles' son Jacques, who is in the middle of his own transition from open-wheel to Sprint Cup cars.

That dominating performance earned him a spot with Bettenhausen Motorsports for the 1997 Champ Car World Series, and his 17th place finish took rookie-of-the-year honors.

For the next seven years, he raced for the famed Forsythe team and won five times. He left Champ Car for the IRL's Red Bull team in 2005, partly because he yearned to race more often on ovals.

He abandoned the IRL after one year and drove for Team Canada in the 2006 A1 Grand Prix season. Later that year, he climbed into his first stock car, in the CASCAR Super Series at Cayuga, Ontario. Starting at the back of the grid, he worked his way to a fifth place finish.

"It was like driving a rental car on steroids," he joked.

In 2007 Carpentier raced a full season in the Daytona Prototype Grand-Am Rolex Series as well as impressing GEM with his Busch Series debut. And by the end of the season, he was accepting a sweater from Lafleur and a full-time Cup ride from Gillett Evernham.

"A year ago I was digging holes on my farm, and now I'm driving a NASCAR Cup car," Carpentier told the *Montreal Gazette*. "It's just so unbelievable how all the planets have aligned for me in such a short time."

In Carpentier's first Champ Car win, at Michigan in 2001, he set a track record by moving up from 21st to edge Dario Franchitti by .024 seconds. Both drivers made their full-season Sprint Cup debuts in 2008.

Above: Carpentier in the Gillette Evernham Motorsports Dodge at Atlanta. The Quebecker has a wealth of racing behind him. About the only thing he hasn't done is compete in drag racing.

Opposite: Carpentier's star has risen quickly, just two years ago he was out of racing and fixing up the family farm in Quebec.

ROBBY GORDON

NO: **7**

BORN:
January 2, 1969

HOMETOWN:
Orange, Calif.

TEAM: **Robby Gordon**

CAR: **Ford**

SPONSOR: **Jim Beam/
Menards/Mapei/
Camping World**

CUP WINS: **3**

CAREER EARNINGS:
$22,957,285

Many stock car drivers like to think they're self-sufficient, yet few actually are. But Robby Gordon is definitely independent, almost to a fault.

In an era when Sprint Cup racing has evolved toward massive garages with all-star driving teams, Gordon has moved in the opposite direction.

As he struggled through the final season of a three-year deal with Richard Childress Racing in 2004, Gordon entered his own team in the Busch Series. Bolstered by a win at Richmond, in 2005 he moved up to Cup racing, where his one-car outfit must compete against the overwhelming resources of the corporate giants.

Fiercely self-reliant, Gordon has inched from his 37th overall in 2005 to 30th the next year and a very respectable 25th in 2007. He continues to attract sponsorship, and in 2007 there were only two races he didn't finish, compared to nine the previous year and 13 the season before.

Since striking out on his own, Gordon has rarely finished in the top 10 of a race (just seven times in his first three years), but he's always been a strong opponent on the track. Many Cup drivers say that if he had more backing, he'd challenge for a top-12 finish every week.

But Gordon likes to do it his way, and he doesn't seem to care if it chafes fans, other drivers or NASCAR officials. A throbbing example of his contrarian nature came during

the inaugural Busch race in Montreal, in early August, 2007.

Gordon and Marcos Ambrose got into a nasty bumping match near the end of the race. Gordon was ordered into 13th, but refused to accept that relegation — arguing that he had planned to protest the decision and officials wouldn't know where to place him unless he finished the race — and on the re-start he crossed the finish line first. Angered NASCAR officials suspended him for the Pocono 500 and eventually placed him on probation until the end of the season.

Searching for the right chemistry, Gordon went through several crew chiefs in 2007 before heading into 2008 with Frank Kerr, with whom he'd worked twice before.

Although his results have improved with more experience as an owner-driver, when he switched back to Ford after six years in Chevrolets, Gordon's 2007 got off to a slow start as the manufacturer struggled with the Car of Tomorrow. It didn't help either that his general manager, John Story, left while Gordon was away competing in the Dakar Rally.

The demanding Dakar holds a special place in Gordon's heart, as does the Indy 500. Gordon finished eighth in the Dakar in 2007, and two years earlier had became the first American ever to win a leg of the famous rally. He had committed fully to the 2008 race and when terrorism concerns prompted the 11th-hour cancellation of the race, Gordon angrily retorted that he was out $4.5 million in expenses.

Clearly, Gordon loves a challenge, as evidenced by his multiple attempts to race NASCAR's Coca-Cola 600 and the Indy 500 on the same day. Rain at Indianapolis thwarted a couple of earlier attempts but in 2002, he was an impressive eighth in the Indy, and 16th in the Cup race.

"I just like to race," he understates.

When Gordon was 17, he and his father won four off-road races and the next year they won the gruelling Baja 1000. He won four straight SCORE/HDRA off-road championships from 1986-89. He raced his first stock car in 1990, when he also won the 24 Hours of Daytona for Roush Racing, and several off-road titles.

Gordon debuted in NASCAR's top series with an 18th-place finish at the 1991 Daytona 500 but made only sporadic Cup appearances until 1997, when he started 20 races for Felix Sabates. He was primarily a CART driver until 2000, when he teamed with John Menard and Mike Held to enter his own car for 17 Winston Cup races. He drove for three owners in 2001, and his win for Childress at New Hampshire led to a permanent ride. In 2003 he won both Cup road races and finished a career-high 16th overall.

With the CoT now leveling the field, look for Gordon to give the big boys a real run for their money.

Gordon led 33 laps near the end of the 1999 Indy 500 but ran out of fuel on the last lap, finishing fourth.

Above: Ryan Newman (12) threads between Sam Hornish (77) and Gordon in the 2008 Daytona 500. Gordon had a good day, placing eighth.

Opposite: A driver who loves a challenge, both on and off the track, Gordon does things his own way. He is also a better racer than most give him credit for.

BOBBY LABONTE

NO: 43

BORN: May 8, 1964

HOMETOWN: Corpus Christi, Tex.

TEAM: Petty Enterprises

CAR: Dodge

SPONSOR: Cheerios/ Betty Crocker

CUP WINS: 21

CAREER EARNINGS: $55,860,859

No matter who their favorite driver happens to be, most stock car fans would love to see a Petty Enterprises car get back into Victory Lane. And they'd love the driver of that car to be Bobby Labonte.

The 2000 Winston Cup champion has the pleasure — and bears the weight — of driving the No. 43 made famous by company icon Richard Petty, a.k.a. the "King."

But when Labonte finished 18th overall in 2007, it was the first time in eight years that the No. 43 had cracked the top 20. Although he didn't have a top-five finish in 2007, after three in 2006, his first year with Petty, Labonte did rise three spots in the standings.

"You can look at the numbers and it's pretty black and white," says Labonte, among the most unflappable personalities in Sprint Cup racing.

"If you finished 18th in points, and you weren't that high the previous season, you have improved. But this sport is more about chemistry than stats. It's about what it takes to get to the end result. What and who are the ingredients that make that happen, and that's why I feel we improved in 2007."

And although that improvement has been measured in the smallest increments, Labonte hopes that a move 70 miles south will result in a more significant move north ... up the standings.

In early 2008 Petty Enterprises left Level Cross, North Carolina, where it had spent nearly 60 years, for Robert Yates Racing's former shop at Mooresville, North Carolina, an area teeming with NASCAR garages.

With the move and expanded facilities, new car chief Raymond Fox coming over from Yates Racing, and crew chief Jeff Meendering arriving from a great run at Hendrick Motorsports, Labonte foresees a brighter future.

"It's going to be beneficial because we're putting people in the right places," he said. "There are people who wouldn't drive all the way to Level Cross to work for us. And having Jeff gives me more confidence, knowing that we're doing all the right things. It will push us a little farther ahead."

And a little more might be all Labonte needs. He got everything he could out of his Dodge in 2007, after the team struggled with the nose of the car, and its overall aerodynamics.

Labonte moved to Petty Enterprises after 11 years at Joe Gibbs Racing because Kyle Petty is one of his best friends and also because he became disenchanted during his final two seasons at JGR. In 2004, for the first time in nine years, he didn't win a race and in 2005 he incurred a whopping 10 DNFs.

That was a long way from his championship run of 2000, when he failed to complete only nine laps over the entire season, won four times and finished in the top-10 in exactly two-thirds of the races.

Over the combined seasons of 2000 and 1999, when he was runner-up to Dale Jarrett, Labonte ran off a stunning 42 top-five finishes in 72 races.

Until a winless streak that began with the first race of 2004 and continued right through 2007, Labonte had run off at least one victory in each of his nine seasons with JGR, and 21 overall.

Winning races is a family tradition, so Labonte feels right at home with the lineage of success at Petty Enterprises.

Labonte's older brother, Terry, won Cup titles 12 years apart, and when he clinched his second one at Atlanta on the final day of the 1996 season, Bobby Labonte was the race winner.

The brothers grew up in Corpus Christi, Texas, but when Bobby was 14 the family moved to North Carolina to advance Terry's racing career.

Below: Labonte (43) in an altercation at Bristol in 2008 with Jamie McMurray, Paul Menard, Ryan Newman and Michael Waltrip. He ended up 38th.

Labonte worked in the garage and pit crews where his brother raced and eventually got into Late Models himself. In 1987 he captured the track title at Caraway Speedway in Asheboro.

After he won the Busch Series title in 1991 and finished second the following year, Labonte got a full-time Cup ride with Bill Davis Racing in 1993. He finished 19th and 21st in two seasons there, before Gibbs tagged him to replace legend Dale Jarrett in the No. 18.

He won three times that year and immediately became a huge fan favorite for his well-grounded attitude. It's a trait that has helped him survive some disappointing results in recent years.

Opposite: From a 1993 start in Cup racing with Bill Davis, Bobby Labonte has won his share of races. He now pilots a Petty Enterprises Dodge, an arrangement born of friendship with Kyle Petty.

MARK MARTIN

NO: **8**

BORN:
January 9, 1959

HOMETOWN:
Batesville, Ark.

TEAM:
Dale Earnhardt, Inc.

CAR: **Chevrolet**

SPONSOR: **U.S. Army**

CUP WINS: **35**

CAREER EARNINGS:
$63,829,009

He is a part-time driver but a full-time star.

Mark Martin has been able to reduce his commitment to Sprint Cup racing and still maintain a razor-sharp competitive edge. Most drivers who had tried that before him, including Bill Elliott and Terry Labonte, were unable to combine an abbreviated racing schedule with top results.

But in 2007, at the age of 48, Martin finished 27th in the drivers standings, despite voluntarily skipping one third of the races. And he turned in 11 top-10 finishes.

He shared his ride at Ginn Racing with Regan Smith, and after the company merged with DEI, Aric Almirola took the seat for the races Martin sat out.

Martin, who had conducted a farewell tour in 2005 before reconsidering, plans to continue with a partial calendar but insists he won't return to a full-time schedule.

"Believe me, I've had opportunity to change that," says Martin who replaces Dale Earnhardt Jr., in the No. 8 at DEI. "I've stuck to my guns 100 percent. I can't think of any scenario that would bring me back full time. I love what I'm doing, and I really feel like I've got the best gig at NASCAR."

Martin had decided to retire after the 2005 season, which was billed as his "Salute to You" tour, offering thanks for the massive fan support he had enjoyed over a quarter-century.

He figured it was a good time to bow out, after rebounding from a disastrous 17th in 2003 to finish fourth overall in 2004.

But a funny thing happened on the way to the sidelines. Martin kept getting older ... and better. In 2004 he didn't make the top-10 until Labor Day, and then he finished fourth. In 2005, which included his first win in 52 races, he went from ninth to fourth in the season's final race, and Jack Roush talked him into postponing his retirement for a year.

Martin did well again in 2006, finishing ninth overall to become one of only three drivers to qualify for the first three Chases of Cup history. He had four top-five finishes in the season's first five races.

And while it was widely anticipated that he would move to a full-time Roush ride in the Craftsman Truck series, he discovered that he didn't want to leave the Cup circuit, or continue with a full-time schedule. So, in October 2006, Martin shocked the stock car world by announcing that he would join MB2 for a part-time ride in 2007.

"At 39 I started to make plans for the future and I realize now that was way too early," Martin said at the time. "I thought that at the age I am right now, I wouldn't be able to compete with these guys. But when you can compete like I have been able to do the last couple of years, against this kind of competition, it's hard to stay away from it."

MB2 had won only two races since it entered Cup racing in 1997, but the arrival of new owner Bobby Ginn gave Martin confidence in the team.

And Martin gave the team confidence in the first race of 2007, when he lost the Daytona 500 by inches to Kevin Harvick. He had four more top-fives that season.

Martin, warmer and far more approachable than the aloof racer he'd been for the first two decades of his career, is expected to be a positive influence on the younger DEI drivers. The serious-minded Martin is often called the racer's racer, or the best stock car driver never to have won a Cup championship.

He's come close, finishing as runner-up four times and losing the 1990 title by 26 points to Dale Earnhardt, the man who founded the company for which he now drives. Another three times, he finished third in the points standing and in the 18 years before he cut back his schedule, he finished out of the top-10 drivers only twice.

"The first time I ever got into a Cup car back in 1981 at North Wilesboro, I was there to win," he says.

And, even on a part-time schedule, he's still there to win.

Opposite: The elder statesman of NASCAR Cup racing has gone to DEI to race a bit, but mostly to foster the next generation.

Below: For Dale Jr. fans, someone else driving the No. 8 car has been a big change. Here's Martin in the 2008 Auto Club 500 at Fontana where he placed 16th.

JAMIE MCMURRAY

NO: 26

BORN: June 3, 1976

HOMETOWN:
Joplin, Mo.

TEAM:
Roush Fenway Racing

CAR: Ford

SPONSOR:
Crown Royal

CUP WINS: 2

CAREER EARNINGS:
$22,993,452

A lot of things happened over the nearly five years it took to complete 166 NASCAR Cup races. But none of those things was a win by Jamie McMurray.

The likeable driver from the Show Me State had struggled to show much to anyone until lucky 07/07/07 (July 7, 2007) when he edged Kyle Busch by a bumper to win the Pepsi 400 at Daytona.

The .005 second differential made it the second-closest race in NASCAR history, but for McMurray, it closed a chasm the size of the Grand Canyon.

He hadn't collected a checkered flag in 166 starts, since early October, 2002, when he made one of the splashiest entries ever into Cup racing.

Sitting in for the injured Sterling Marlin at Chip Ganassi Racing with Felix Sabates, McMurray, then a Busch Series regular, won at Charlotte in just his second Cup start.

It was the first time in the modern era, and just the 11th in the long history of Cup racing, that a driver collected a victory within his first two starts. And before another month had passed, McMurray had also won his first two Busch races.

McMurray seemed poised for stardom, but his career leveled off and the long winning drought became a burden. He left Ganassi-Sabates for Jack Roush Racing in 2006, hoping for a change of fortunes, but it took another year and a half before he found Victory Lane again.

"I savoured it," he said, admitting that he cried afterward. "When I won Charlotte, it was an odd circumstance because I was subbing for Sterling. You were just trying to be grateful, because you were in someone else's ride and you didn't get to enjoy it with your team.

"This time I got to enjoy it with my team."

Still, McMurray was being eyed as one of the drivers Roush might have to cut when forced to reduce to four teams for the 2010 season.

After finishing just out of the Chase at 11th in 2004 and 12th in 2005, McMurray plummeted to 25th in 2006, his first season with Roush.

He spent that off-season working on "the mental side, on just being prepared," he said. "It's easier when things go well to be positive than it is when you went through what I went through."

Soon after an accident in the 2007 Daytona 500, McMurray had five top-10 finishes within seven races and was in 10th place overall. He missed the Chase yet again, though, with his 17th-place finish. He had that welcome victory and eight other top 10s, but 11 finishes of 30th or worse spoke to major inconsistency.

Heading into 2008, McMurray knew he was under the gun and hired a personal trainer to build up his strength and endurance for the demanding Cup grind.

Trying to rekindle a little magic, McMurray took part in KartWeek at Daytona in the last week of 2007. He had begun his racing career on Missouri cart tracks at the age of seven. He owned four national cart championships by the time he was 16 and won the 1991 world championship.

In 1992 he moved into late models and eventually ran NASCAR Dodge Weekly Series races at several tracks. In 1997 he captured the track championship at I-44 Speedway, and he also competed in the Grand American Late Model Class until 1998.

He moved into Craftsman Trucks for five races in 1999, while also racing in the NASCAR Midwest Series, then had a full-time Truck ride in 2000. That year, he also began three years of full-time Busch Series racing, which peaked with his two victories in late 2002.

McMurray's full-time Cup ride began in 2003 where he finished 13th in driver's points to win rookie of the year ahead of Greg Biffle, his future teammate at Roush Fenway Racing.

Roush-Fenway enjoyed a hot start in 2008, despite penalty troubles concerning Carl Edwards. For McMurray to keep himself in the mix, he will have to make sure that every ride counts for something for the talented Roush-Fenway team.

McMurray accomplished his victories in each of NASCAR's three national series in reverse of the usual order: first winning a Cup race, then Busch and then Craftsman.

Opposite: McMurray started with Chip Ganassi in 2002 and went over to Roush in 2006, where his fortunes started to change for the better.

Below: This minor punch-up at Bristol looks more like a cruise-night gathering of Cup cars featuring McMurray (left), Paul Menard, Ryan Newman, and Arci Almirola. McMurray ended up 43rd.

CASEY MEARS

NO: 5

BORN: March 12, 1978

HOMETOWN: Bakersfield, Calif.

TEAM: Hendrick Motorsports

CAR: Chevrolet

SPONSOR: Kellogg's/CARQUEST

CUP WINS: 1

CAREER EARNINGS: $21,639,66

Just how much can a monkey weigh? If it's hitching a ride on your body, about five tons, says Casey Mears.

"I just had a 10,000 pound gorilla jump off my back," Mears laughed after he won NASCAR's longest race, the Coca-Cola 600, in late May, 2007.

After more than four full seasons, and 155 starts, of Cup racing without a victory, Mears knew the stock car world was wondering aloud whether he really had the stuff to win.

Taking his first win on Memorial Day weekend made silencing his critics all the more satisfying. His famous uncle, Rick Mears, was synonymous with the last weekend in May, winning the Indianapolis 500 a record-tying four times.

"I watched my uncle win four races on this day and, man, what a special day just because of that," said Mears, whose father, Roger, also raced twice at the famous Brickyard.

It was all the more special because of Mears' strategy. Under hot and sunny conditions, with other drivers complaining about the hard tires, Mears gambled with his fuel level and ran out of gas just seconds after crossing the finish line.

His first Cup victory brought some welcome grounding to the shifting sands of his career. He was on his third different car in three years.

Mears' victory was among the 18 captured in 2007 by powerful Hendrick Motorsports, which he joined at the beginning of the season after four years with Chip Ganassi.

He was looking for better results, and the chance to share a garage with good friends and fellow Californians Jimmie Johnson and Jeff Gordon. But while those two dominated the Chase, Mears did not qualify, finishing 15th overall, a drop of one place from his final season at Ganassi.

But Mears' five finishes in the top-five were as many as he had in the two preceding years combined.

After Kyle Busch departed, owner Rick Hendrick shifted Mears to the former crew of the No. 5 car, with Alan Gustafson as crew chief. After two different crews in his final two years at Ganassi, that meant Mears was entering 2008 with his fourth crew chief in four seasons.

"Obviously at some point it's going to be nice to have a good couple of years in a row with the same crew chief, and all the same sponsors and just kind of build the relationship and carry it over into the next season," Mears said. "And we should get that now."

Mears has been in stock cars only since the final weeks of the 2001 season when he finished ninth in an ARCA race at Talladega. After consulting with his uncle and father, he turned away from the prospect of a good career with IRL or CART, for a 2002 Busch Series contract with Welliver-Jessel Motorsports.

He had started racing BMX events when he was only four years old. Spurred by the competitive urge, he switched to ATVs at Bakersfield,

then took up go-karts before moving into Super-Lites off-road racing when he was 14. When he won at Mesa Marin Raceway at the age of 16, he was the second-youngest winner, ever, of a Jim Russell USAC Triple Crown event. A year later he was series champion.

He moved into Indy Lite cars in 1996, was second in the points race in 1999 and the next year won the Grand Prix of Houston.

But by 2002 Mears had committed to being a full-time stock car driver. He finished only 21st in the Busch Series for Welliver-Jessell, so it was considered a gamble when Chip Ganassi and Felix Sabates coaxed him into a Cup car for the 2003 season.

Mears struggled in his rookie year, failing to finish 10 times, never ending in the top 10, and ranking 35th overall. But in 2003 he jumped to 22nd, with a fourth place at Watkins Glen, and nine top-10s, while slashing his DNFs to three.

He was 22nd again in 2005 but leapt to 14th in 2006, while winning his first national series race, a Busch Series triumph at Chicagoland, where he coasted home out of gas, a preview of his first Cup win a year later.

Midway through the 2006 season, Mears announced that he would leave Ganassi, and was soon signed by Hendrick Motorsports to replace Brian Vickers.

"My decision has been based strictly on where I feel I can perform better," he said.

In 2006 Mears, Scott Nixon and Dan Wheldon teamed up to win the Rolex 24-Hours of Daytona, making Mears the first full-time NASCAR Cup driver to win the Rolex 24.

Opposite: A former successful open-wheel racer, Mears has made the transition to stock cars rather than going into the IRL.

Below: Mears had some problems in the 2008 Daytona 500 in his Hendrick Motorsports Chevy. An accident ended his day in 35th.

JUAN PABLO MONTOYA

NO: 42

BORN:
September 20, 1975

HOMETOWN:
Bogota, Colombia

TEAM:
Chip Ganassi Racing with Felix Sabates

CAR: Dodge

SPONSOR:
Texaco/Halvoline/
Juicy Fruit/Big Red

CUP WINS: 1

CAREER EARNINGS:
$5,390,445

It was not easy, and it was not always friendly, but Juan Pablo Montoya opened the floodgates.

In the wake of Montoya's rookie-of-the-year honors, a number of other big names have made the switch to Sprint Cup racing.

But Montoya has always been one of a kind. Just because he was able to finish 20th overall, and win Busch and Nextel Cup races in his debut season, that doesn't automatically mean others will be as successful.

By the time Montoya opened the 2007 Cup calendar with a commendable 19th in the Daytona 500, he had already won seven Formula-One races, the Formula 3000 drivers championship, the CART championship, the

24 Hours of Daytona and the most prestigious open-wheel races in North America and Europe: the Indy 500 and the Grand Prix of Monaco.

Still, Montoya had difficulties adapting to the bigger, heavier machines of NASCAR which have less grip on the road.

"I'll tell you, it's a handful," Montoya said after his first full season on ovals. "The car really keeps you busy."

Always an aggressive driver known for daring passes, Montoya absorbed his share of criticism during his rookie year.

Tony Stewart lambasted him at Texas in April; Kevin Harvick angrily confronted him in August after their cars collided late in the

Watkins Glen race; and he was put on probation after he made a rude gesture to a Speed Channel camera.

And at the Busch series race in Mexico City Montoya earned the wrath of teammate Scott Pruett, whom he spun with on an inside passing attempt on his way to his first career win driving stock. Not surprisingly, it was on a road course, as was his first ever Cup win, at Sonoma in June, and it ushered in a new era.

That victory, off a pass of Jamie McMurray, was the first Cup win by a foreign driver since Canadian Earl Ross, 33 years earlier. It was the first checkered flag for Chip Ganassi Racing with Felix Sabates since McMurray won in 2002.

"I think this is a cool moment," Montoya said of his victory. "And it's a major moment for NASCAR."

And it made Montoya the only driver other than Mario Andretti to cash major victories in stock, Champ, Indy, Grand-Am and F-1 cars.

Montoya grew up around racing in Bogota, Colombia. His uncle, Diego Montoya, was a star of North American GT racing in the 1980s, and his father, Pablo, raced go-karts locally, often taking his son with him to the track.

He began racing karts at the age of eight, and eventually won the Kart Junior World Championship. His goal was to make it to Formula One, and by 1997 he was racing International Formula 3000 cars. The next season he won the FIA championship with a record point total.

Ganassi talked him into joining his CART team in 1999, and he stunned the racing fraternity by winning rookie of the year and the overall championship. After he won the Indy 500 in 2000, he left CART for his lifelong dream: an F-1 ride with Williams.

In just his third race, at the Grand Prix of Brazil, he pushed legendary Michael Schumacher off the road, kick-starting a reputation for outrageous overtaking maneuvers.

When he left Williams after the 2004 season, he had four wins — including the Grand Prix of Monaco — 23 podium results, and two third-place finishes in the points race.

A move to Team McLaren/Mercedes didn't pay off, although he won the 2005 British Grand Prix. When he failed to finish five of the first 10 races of 2006, he announced he would leave at the end of the season to drive a Sprint Cup car for Ganassi and Felix Sabates.

Although there were still eight F-1 races left, McLaren released him from his contract, and he got into the final Cup race of the year, finishing 34th, after a fiery crash.

In 2007 he had the victory at Sonoma, and five other top-10s, but also finished below 30th in 11 races, indicating how much more difficult it is to keep a stock car running consistently.

"We had everything, it was up and down," Montoya said of his stock car inititation. "But I'm finally enjoying racing again."

The Formula Smiles Foundation, established by Connie and Juan Pablo Montoya, has helped 10,000 underprivileged children in Columbia have access to athletic facilities.

Above: Montoya at speed with Jimmie Johnson at the 2008 Daytona 500, where he took 32nd. After racing at the pinnacle of open-wheel, the Columbian native has said he finds stock car racing a challenge. "It's a handful."

Opposite: This former CART and Formula One driver became the first foreign driver to win a Cup race in 33 years.

DAVID RAGAN

NO: **6**

BORN:
December 24, 1985

HOMETOWN:
Unadilla, Ga.

TEAM:
Roush Fenway Racing

CAR: **Ford**

SPONSOR: **AAA**

CUP WINS: **0**

CAREER EARNINGS:
$5,126,318

David Ragan is learning that to make giant strides forward you sometimes have to take a small step backward.

So he's determined to learn how to recognize when to hold 'em and when to fold 'em.

"We had to slow him down a bit so that he could finish races," team owner Jack Roush said after Ragan's 2007 debut season, when the 21-year-old rookie led all Cup drivers in spins and crashes.

Ragan, who had enough potential that Roush tagged him to replace Mark Martin, would often fail to identify his limits during a specific race and over-drive, leading to a wreck or a low finish.

"Just being fast is only about half of it," Ragan

concedes. "There are things where I need to be better and that's going to be the difference between being 20th every week and 10th. If you've got a 10th-place car, make sure you finish 10th with it."

Still, despite his rookie mistakes, Ragan finished a respectable 23rd overall in his first year, and second in the rookie standings to Juan Pablo Montoya. He was also one of only five drivers to run complete Cup and Busch schedules, and the blueprint called for him to do the same double duty in Sprint Cup and Nationwide series for 2008, and perhaps beyond.

Roush feels that the enthusiastic Ragan, a graduate of the company's "Gong Show" development program, will soon win a Nationwide Series points championship and crack the top 20 in Sprint Cup ranks.

He certainly began his rookie season as if he was headed for big things. Starting 35th at the 2007 Daytona, Ragan played it safe all the way through the disaster-filled race to finish fifth overrall. He was 16th the following week at California, and later admitted that he began thinking Cup racing wasn't going to be as difficult as he had anticipated.

But reality set in and he didn't have a second top-five result until early September, 25 races later, and had to wait until the final race of the season to record his third top-10 (10th at Homestead) of the season.

On the secondary Busch — now Nationwide — series, he had four top-fives and took two poles, but didn't win a race.

By placing a solid fifth overall in Busch and taking rookie-of-the-year honors — the third in a row for Roush-Fenway Racing — Ragan felt he had accomplished two of his three goals in his first full season of big-time racing. But he was deeply disappointed that he had fallen short in the Cup rookie standings.

"We just didn't perform like we wanted in the last half of the season," he said.

Ragan grew up around major tracks. His father, Ken, was a veteran of different NASCAR series and made 30 Cup starts between 1982 and 1990, mostly in a car owned by David's grandfather, Marvin Ragan.

David Ragan started competing at the age of 11 in the Bandolero Series at Atlanta Motor Speedway. In his sophomore season he captured a dozen features and he eventually worked his way up to a national championship.

In 2002 Ragan got his first NASCAR experience, with seven Late Model starts on various North Carolina tracks.

Two years later, at 18, he became eligible for NASCAR national divisions and made 10 Craftsman Truck starts for Fiddleback racing. He also ran some ARCA events, landing a second-place finish at Kentucky Motor Speedway.

Ragan began to make his career move in 2005, pocketing a dozen top-10 finishes in 28 ARCA races, with three poles and his first major win, at Georgia's Lanier National Speedway. He also got three Busch series starts and landed a Craftsman Truck ride for 2006, through Roush's development program.

He made 19 truck starts for Roush in 2006, with eight top-10 finishes, and got his first taste of Cup racing in late-season starts at Dover (42nd) and Martinsville (25th). In the Martinsville race, Ragan crashed with Ken Schrader prompting legend Tony Stewart to call him "a dart without feathers." NASCAR wouldn't let him race the following week at Atlanta.

Despite Ragan's relative inexperience, and against widespread skepticism, Jack Roush promoted him to the Cup circuit for 2007. The results were mixed but Roush, who has an eye for young talent, was not discouraged with his enthusiastic young protégé.

"Unfortunately every rookie has to have a rookie season," he said.

Above: While he finished fifth in the 2007 Daytona 500, Ragan had some issues in the 2008 race in his AAA-sponsored Ford, taking 42nd.

Opposite: Ragan's 2007 debut with Roush Fenway Racing saw the rookie running in both Cup and Busch Series racing.

ELLIOT SADLER

NO: 19
BORN: April 30, 1975
HOMETOWN: Emporia, Va.
TEAM: Gillett Evernham Motorsports
CAR: Dodge
SPONSOR: Best Buy
CUP WINS: 3
CAREER EARNINGS: $34,184,869

A long winless streak and harsh self-criticism can be a lethal combination, so Elliott Sadler had to cut himself some slack.

"I've matured a lot," says the Gillett Evernham Motorsports driver. "If this had happened to me in my first couple of years of racing, I'd have probably just gone crazy."

Sadler, who has sometimes been so hard on himself that it severely affected his confidence, came into the 2008 season off his worst standing in the points race in seven years and without a win in 119 Cup starts.

His last victory was at California in September, 2004, the year he barged into the upper tier of Cup racing with two wins, and qualified

for the inaugural Chase in sixth spot, before finishing ninth overall.

But since then he has not made the Chase, and in the middle of the 2006 season fled Robert Yates Racing for Evernham, where he finished an undistinguished 22nd in 2006 and 25th in 2007.

In 2007, for the first time since 2000, his sophomore Cup year at Wood Brothers Racing, he did not have a single top-five finish.

"It was the most frustrating season I've had in 25 years of racing," he said.

The entire garage had difficulty adapting to the Car of Tomorrow, and Sadler himself struggled with the adjustment to Dodges after driving Fords at RYR. And, many times, he

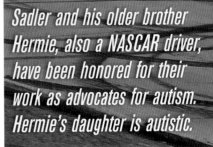

Sadler and his older brother Hermie, also a NASCAR driver, have been honored for their work as advocates for autism. Hermie's daughter is autistic.

simply did not drive well.

Gillett Evernham responded by beefing up the experience on his crew, making Rodney Childers the team director, and by promising that competition director, Mark McArdle, would work more closely with Sadler.

"He knows that he's got the ability and we want to put him in the race cars which can win," company founder Ray Evernham said. "These are the years that he should perform and make his mark."

Sadler has endured a winless drought before and emerged as a front-runner. Early in 2001 he gave the Wood Brothers their first victory in eight years with a win at Bristol. But he had only three other top-five finishes in his remaining 60-plus races with the company, before he shifted to RYR in 2003 in hopes of better results.

At Yates Racing, Sadler replaced departing legend Ricky Rudd who, ironically, went over to the Wood Brothers. He had nine top-10s in his first season for RYR and finished 22nd overall.

Then, in 2004, he vaulted all the way to ninth in the points race, and indications were that he'd become a legitimate championship contender. In 2005 he was in third place through 16 races, before he plummeted down the standings, missed the Chase by one position and dropped to 13th overall. By the middle of the next season he was at Evernham Motorsports.

Sadler's recent difficulties are at odds with his varied and successful athletic past.

Growing up in Virginia, where his father, Herman, raced Late Model stocks, Sadler excelled at six different sports and received a basketball scholarship to James Madison University. A knee injury curtailed his basketball career and allowed him to concentrate on his budding racing career.

He had started in go-karts at the age of seven, won the state championship at eight and eventually rang up more than 200 kart victories.

Sadler was only 18 when he started competing regularly in NASCAR's Dodge Weekly series. Just two years later, he won six races in a row and 13 overall on the way to the track title at highly-competitive South Boston Speedway.

After two years of a limited schedule of Busch racing, Sadler moved full time to NASCAR's second-tier national series in 1997 and took the pole in the season opener at Daytona. He won at Nazareth in just his 13th Busch start and finished fifth in the points championship.

He won five times in 76 Busch starts before graduating to full-time Cup racing with the Wood Brothers in 1999. After four years there and another three-and-a-half with Robert Yates, he joined Kasey Kahne at Evernham.

While still deeply concerned that he hasn't climbed back into the elite ranks for Gillett Evernham, Sadler says, "I realize that I can't put the car on my back and tote it around."

Although he'd probably like to.

Opposite: Sadler first went Cup racing with the Woods Brothers in 1999. Now he's driving a Gillett Evernham Dodge.

Sadler getting his Dodge serviced during the Gatorade Duels 150 at Daytona, 2008.

REED SORENSON

NO: 41

BORN:
February 5, 1986

HOMETOWN:
Davidson, N.C.

TEAM:
Chip Ganassi Racing
with Felix Sabates

CAR: Dodge

SPONSOR: Target

CUP WINS: 0

CAREER EARNINGS:
$8,234,141

When Chip Ganassi looks at Reed Sorenson, he hopes he sees the future of Sprint Cup racing.

Sorenson is the low-key voice among the brand-new Cup choir that owners Ganassi and Felix Sabates have been assembling since 2005. Celebrated teammates, open-wheel transfers Juan Pablo Montoya and Dario Franchiti, have attracted far more attention than Sorenson who was raised on stock cars in the shadow of Atlanta Motor Speedway— and that's okay.

While he is nearly a dozen years younger than his famous teammates, he entered the 2008 season with two years' experience, twice as much experience as both men combined.

"I don't think it's intimidating to be surrounded by two Indy 500 winners. In fact I think it's pretty cool," Sorenson said. "We need to take the next step of moving from a team that finishes 20th to one that earns a spot in the Chase. If we do that, we'll create our own headlines."

Ganassi says that Sorenson is cocky on the race track, but shy in real life.

In 2006 Sorenson finished 24th in the points standings, and fourth on the rookie chart. He moved up two spots in 2007 and, although he was still searching for his first Cup victory, he had three top-five finishes, compared to just one in his debut season.

And at Indianapolis he became the youngest driver, at 21, ever to win a pole. The previous

record had been set by 22-year-old Rex Mays for the Indy 500, 72 years earlier.

If the Sprint Cup held most of its races at Atlanta, Sorenson might challenge for the driver's championship. In 2006 he finished 10th in the spring race, for the first top-10 finish of his career. In 2007 he held the lead there in March, but ran out of gas to finish up the track, and in the July race he moved from a 32nd starting position to finish third, the best result of his young career.

The comfort level with Atlanta is understandable, since he grew up in nearby Peachtree and became familiar with Georgia tracks watching his father, Brad, race on weekends.

"Racing has been part of me and my family for as long as I can remember," he said.

As their son became more deeply interested in racing, Brad and Becky Sorenson sought counsel from other racing parents on how to best further their son's career.

And that career was a promising one.

Starting at age six, he raced quarter-midgets for five seasons, winning a national championship in 1997. The same year he set qualifying records in both the east and west coast nationals. By the time he was finished he held records at 15 different tracks.

He was no less dominant when he moved to Legend cars, the reduced-scale replicas of NASCAR modifieds, winning a stunning 83

times in 183 starts.

By 2002 he had joined ARCA and reaped seven top-10 finishes in his eight starts. The following season, while still in high school, Sorenson became the youngest rookie of the year in ASA history, with seven top-fives and 14 top-10s in just 17 starts. Ganassi was suitably impressed and signed him to a development contract.

In the jam-packed 2004 season, Sorenson graduated from Woodward Academy, won his first ASA race, and could have won the driver's title but for an accident near the end of the final race. He had three ARCA starts, winning one and finishing second and fourth in the others.

Ganassi also gave him five Busch starts that season, and when he responded with three top-10 finishes, Sorenson earned a full-time Busch ride for 2005. He won by 14 seconds at Nashville in just his 11th start. He won again at Gateway and finished fourth overall, losing a narrow rookie-of-the-year title chase to Carl Edwards.

Sorenson ran both Busch and Cup in 2006, and since his rookie year has made steady progress. And with a work ethic like Sorenson's, and a vow to work harder on his weak spots, it is all music to Chip Ganassi's ears.

In 2007 Sorenson started his own charity golf tournament; in October he drove a pink Cup car in support of the fight against breast cancer.

Above: Sorenson testing at Phoenix in March of 2008 in the Chip Ganassi Racing with Felix Sabates Dodge. He says he is not intimidated by his older, more experienced teammates.

Opposite: Sorenson has a solid background of ARCA and ASA stock car racing. His teammates now include two world-class drivers, Juan Pablo Montoya, and Dario Franchitti.

J.J. YELEY

NO: 96

BORN:
October 5, 1976

HOMETOWN:
Phoenix, Ariz.

TEAM:
Hall of Fame Racing

CAR: Toyota

SPONSOR: DLP HDTV

CUP WINS: 0

CAREER EARNINGS:
$9,408,564

J.J. Yeley has gone from being led to being the leader.

When Dale Earnhardt Jr. announced in the middle of the 2007 Cup season that he was leaving DEI, the ripple effect spread all the way to Yeley.

Earnhardt Jr. dislodged Kyle Busch for 2008 at Hendrick Motorsport. In turn, Busch was hired by Joe Gibbs Racing, where Yeley was beginning to realize some of his vast potential, running in the shadow cast by championship contenders Tony Stewart and Denny Hamlin.

Busch's impending arrival left Yeley out in the cold, but after weighing offers from Richard Childress and Robert Yates, he made a bold choice. In September 2007 Yeley

announced that he was gambling on the single-entry Hall of Fame Racing team.

Hall of Fame, started by pro football legends Troy Aikman and Roger Staubach, had just been sold to Jeff Moorad, managing partner of the Arizona Diamondbacks baseball team, and fellow Diamondbacks executive Tom Garfinkle.

They were promising to invest heavily in the team and add a full-test team in preparation for a second Cup entry in 2009.

As Yeley, an Arizona native, explained, "I just think this is going to be the best fit to be the most comfortable for my career."

The biggest change wasn't that Yeley was switching from a football-oriented owner to baseball-oriented ones but that he would get all the focus instead of standing third in line.

And there would still be a strong connection to Joe Gibbs Racing, which is to provide the chassis and new Toyota engines for HoF.

"Because this is a one-car team, obviously they're not going to have the resources some of the other teams do," Yeley said. "But because they get their cars from JGR everything is familiar to me, and that's important."

He replaced Tony Raines who, in the 2007 season, finished 29th overall, the same ranking Yeley held in 2006, his rookie season. Yeley had climbed to 21st in 2007, which included a runner-up finish at the Coca-Cola 600 and winning the pole in Michigan.

While he had only three top-10 results, he was showing the skills that made J.D. Gibbs pluck him from USAC ranks to race Busch cars in 2004.

Yeley is the son of a legendary midget racer, Jack "Cactus" Yeley, who won seven Arizona Midget Racing Association titles and was two-time World of Outlaws midget champion. The younger Yeley spent the summers of his youth traveling to tracks throughout the far west and mid-west.

"When I was 12 or so I'd sneak into the pit area and groove the race tires, do things that I saw the adults doing," Yeley recalls.

He started in the Arizona Quarter-Midget Racing Association when he was 10 years old and when he was 14 he got into midget racing by using a forged birth certificate. At 16 he was the youngest driver ever granted a USAC license.

When 18-year-old Yeley got his first victory, in a sprint car at Chico, California, he was the youngest winner in SCRA history. He moved up to the USAC in 1997, but also tried some IndyCar racing in 2008, qualifying for the Indy 500 and finishing a credible ninth.

He lacked funding for IRL, though, and concentrated on the USAC. He won the Sprint Car championship in 2001 and in 2002 won the Silver Crown Championship.

That set the stage for one of the most outstanding seasons in USAC history, when Yeley won 24 races in 2003, breaking A.J. Foyt's record by five wins. He also joined Tony Stewart in being the only two drivers to win the USAC Triple crown of Midget, Sprint and Silver crown titles.

Yeley ran 17 Busch series races for JGR in 2004, his first NASCAR experience. By 2006 he was signed to drive the No. 18 Cup car full time, but by the fall of 2007 he had been shunted aside and committed to HoF.

"I had a good relationship with Gibbs, but my job here is to win races, make the Chase and make them regret letting me go," he says.

Yeley was 21 when he ran in the Indy 500 in 1998, at that time he was the youngest driver who'd ever started the famous race.

Opposite: Yeley was a Sprint and Midget car star before getting into a Joe Gibbs Racing Busch car in 2004.

Yeley, who began Cup racing two years ago, has risen steadily in driver points each year. Now he's racing with the Hall of Fame Racing Team in a Toyota, shown here at Bristol in 2008, where Yeley took 25th.

A.J. ALLMENDINGER

NO: 84

BORN:
December 16, 1981

HOMETOWN:
Los Gatos, Calif.

TEAM:
Red Bull Racing

CAR: Toyota

SPONSOR: Red Bull

CUP WINS: 0

CAREER EARNINGS:
$1,316,980

Allendinger's Cup debut was not stellar as he finished with eight accidents in 17 starts.

A.J. Allmendinger summarized his rookie Cup year with his usual mix of humor and self-criticism.

"I'm pretty low on the learning curve," he said of his 2007 season. "For a while, a good weekend was if I didn't wreck, because I didn't know what I was doing."

In his debut season away from open-wheel racing, Allmendinger was engaged in eight accidents in 17 starts.

It was a trying initiation into the NASCAR world, as his fledgling team had no points to carry over and had to qualify for every starting grid. With his car in qualifying trim on Fridays, even when he qualified for Sunday he was behind other teams that had used qualifying laps to get into racing trim.

With a new team, a rookie Cup manufacturer in Toyota, and severe adjustments to NASCAR racing, it's no wonder Allmendinger's best finish in his rookie season was 15th, late in the season.

But Allmendinger has hit deep potholes before and been able to rebound spectacularly. For instance, four races into the 2006 Champ Car season, RuSport shockingly fired him in favor of 2002 series champion Cristiano da Matta. But Forsythe Championship Racing picked him up and he immediately won his first three races, and five in his nine starts.

Still, Forsythe let him go near the end of the season, and Allmendinger made the jump to NASCAR. He ran three Craftsmen's Truck races for Bill Davis Racing, including a fifth-place finish at Talladega, and signed with Red Bull in late October.

That wasn't much preparation for a full Cup season, and it took four qualifying attempts for Allmendinger to start his first race, at Bristol.

"I used to think Champ Car was tough to drive," he said after finishing 40th. "But 500 laps around this place? That's a lot of work."

After a stellar karting career, in which he was two-time International Karting Federation Grand National champion, he won six of 10 races in the 2002 Barber Dodge Pro Series, tying the record for most victories and winning the series championship by an unprecedented 68 points.

That dominating performance got him a ride with RuSport in the 2003 Toyota Atlantic Series and he won eight times, a rookie record. He became the second-youngest points champion in series history.

The RuSport team moved to Champ Car in 2004, and he had five top-six placings in the final six races to become the first American-born driver since 1991 to win rookie of the year. He finished fifth overall in 2005 and seemed destined to become the American star Champ needed when RuSport let him go early in 2006 and Forsythe looked elsewhere, despite his brilliant results.

Toyota is hoping that open-wheel's loss is NASCAR's gain. But as 2007 showed, it's a steep learning curve for both driver and manufacturer.

DARIO FRANCHITTI

NO: 40

BORN: May 12, 1973

HOMETOWN:
Edinburgh, Scotland

TEAM:
Chip Ganassi Racing
with Felix Sabates

CAR: Dodge

SPONSOR: Target

CUP WINS: 0

CAREER EARNINGS: 0

Franchitti is hoping to make the transition from open-wheel to stock cars with minimum difficulty, with help from teammate Juan Pablo Montoya.

It's wise to listen to Mario Andretti – the winner of the Indy 500, the Daytona 500 and the F-1 world championship.

So, when he says that Dario Franchitti should be able to be successful in NASCAR because "he is a very patient guy and it might play to his strengths. He's got 500-mile races to get the car dialed in," he's probably right.

In 2007 the veteran Franchitti won his first Indy 500, and the IRL championship, but at the end of the most successful season he was bound for NASCAR to replace David Stremme at Chip Ganassi Racing with Felix Sabates.

It should be a more fluid transition for Franchitti than for many of the open-wheelers who are migrating to NASCAR, because the Ganassi garage worked out many of the bugs when Juan Pablo Montoya made a similar jump in 2007.

"Juan made a big sales pitch to me, so if it doesn't work out I'll blame him," Franchitti laughed.

Franchitti has more U.S. open-wheel victories than any other driver from Great Britain and has long been associated with

the Andrettis, one of American racing's royal names. And it doesn't hurt the recognition factor that his wife is actor/singer Ashley Judd.

Franchitti is of Italian descent but was born in Scotland and grew up in West Lothian where he began his racing career in go-karts.

By the time he moved to the British Formula Vauxhall Lotus series to train under the legendary Jackie Stewart in 1992, he had won two British junior Kart crowns, the Scottish senior and junior titles, and taken four checkered flags in the British Junior Formula Vauxhall Series.

Franchitti won the Formula Vauxhuall Lotus driver's championship in his second season, and then moved to British Formula 3 and eventually to the FIA International Touring Car Championship, finishing fourth for Mercedes in 1996. When the ITC ceased operations, Mercedes moved him into Champ Cars for Paul Hogan.

In 1998 he was signed by Team KOOL Green, Andretti Green's predecessor. That began a spectacular decade in open-wheel racing in which he won 18 times, took 17 poles, was a narrow second to Montoya in the 1999 Champ standings and fourth in the 2005 IRL driver's championship.

After securing the 2007 IRL title when he got an extra lap of fuel to pass coasting Scott Dixon at Chicagoland in September, Franchitti eased into NASCAR. He finished 17th at an ARCA Series race at Talladega in early October, 2007, and 33rd in a Craftsman Truck Series race later that month. He began his full-time Cup career in 2008.

"These cars move around all over the place," he told a British newspaper after his first Cup testing. "They are unbelievably tricky to set up and I can't see too many of the Americans sharing their secrets with a newcomer.

"I'll get there in the end, but nobody expects me to be winning straight away."

SAM HORNISH JR.

NO: 77

BORN: July 2, 1979

HOMETOWN:
Bryan, Ohio

TEAM:
Penske Racing

CAR: Dodge

SPONSOR: Mobil 1

CUP WINS: 0

CAREER EARNINGS:
$126,325

Former IRL champ Hornish Jr. still races for Roger Penske, but he's changed divisions.

Sam Hornish Jr. is in the hot seat, in more ways than one.

"The physical effort of driving these cars is very great, because it's like you're doing it in a sauna," the former Indy 500 winner said as he was making his transition from open-wheel racing to NASCAR in 2007.

Hornish Jr. also feels another kind of heat: the pressure to produce for team owner Roger Penske, who moved him from the IRL side of the business to a full-time Sprint Cup ride alongside stars Kurt Busch and Ryan Newman.

Penske transferred Busch's owner points to Hornish Jr. so the Cup rookie didn't have the extra burden of qualifying for the first five races of 2008.

And qualifying had proven difficult for the three-time IRL champion. In an eight-race Cup experiment in the fall of 2007, he was unable to make the Sunday grid in his first six attempts, and finally earned starts in the season's last two races, finishing 30th and 37th.

"Well, now I've got twice as much Cup experience as I had before," he quipped after his second start.

Hornish Jr. has said that while Indy Cars might be much tougher to handle for one or two laps, in the long term a Cup race is far more punishing because of "the temperatures you face in the car and the amount of footwork you are doing. Plus there are 43 cars so there is nowhere to relax."

Hornish doesn't relax much, anyway. He's been a busy and successful racer ever since he first entered go-kart competition at the age of 11 in his hometown of Defiance, Ohio. He eventually joined the World Karting Association and in 1994 won the U.S. and Canadian grand championships.

After learning the trade for a family-owned team in the Formula Ford 2000 Series, Hornish Jr. graduated to Shank Racing in the Toyota Atlantic Series in 1999, and won rookie of the year.

PDM hired him for the IRL in 2000, and the following season he switched to Panther Racing. He won five races, including his first two starts and sped away with his first IRL championship. When Penske switched from Champ to IRL in 2001, bringing elite level competition, Hornish Jr. was still able to defend his title.

Penske hired Hornish Jr. for the 2003 season when Gil de Ferran retired and he won his first race for his new employer.

In 2006, on the way to becoming the first three-time IRL champion, he captured the Indy 500 in the final 300 yards over Marco Andretti. He was the first winner of the legendary race ever to make a pass on the final lap.

That same season, Penske put him into the final two Busch races, and he suffered two wrecks in the unfamiliar cars.

"It's going to be a long uphill process," he says. "This could be the biggest mistake I ever made or the best thing I every did."

BRIAN VICKERS

NO: 83

BORN:
October 24, 1983

HOMETOWN:
Thomasville, N.C.

TEAM: Red Bull

CAR: Toyota

SPONSOR: Red Bull

CUP WINS: 1

CAREER EARNINGS:
$14,663,084

After five years of Cup racing, Vickers took a win at Talladega in his last year at Hendrick Motorsports. He is now driving a Red Bull Toyota.

Brian Vickers has been a Cup fixture for so long, it's easy to forget that entering the 2008 season he was only 24 years old.

The cerebral racer from North Carolina was already a three-year veteran by the time he joined Team Red Bull in time for Toyota's Cup debut in 2007.

With no guaranteed spot on owners' points, Vickers failed to qualify for 13 of the season's 36 races, failed to finish six others and had only one top-five result. That fifth place at the Coca-Cola 600 was a first for Toyota. His 10th-place finish in the season's second race at California was the manufacturer's inaugural top-10 in Cup racing, but neither made up for not qualifying for the Daytona 500, and a lowly 38th standing in the points race.

"It was a tough year working with a new team and a new manufacturer, so you could say we were battling many things," Vickers said.

But the future seemed far brighter when he finished 12th in the 2008 Daytona 500, working his way up from 23rd on the starting grid.

In late June 2006, Vickers announced that by

"mutual decision" he would leave his four-year relationshp with Hendrick Motorsports for Toyota at the end of the season.

Ironically, Vickers landed his first Cup victory three months later when he bumped past Hendrick teammate Jimmie Johnson to win at Talladega. Johnson's crew chief, Chad Knaus, fumed that Vickers "ran out of talent" before winning.

Lack of talent has never been one of Vickers' shortcomings, though. His accomplishments have usually out-raced his birth certificate.

He started go-kart racing at the age of 10 and before his 15th birthday had four North Carolina State kart championships and three national championships.

Moving up to the Allison Legacy Car Series, he rang up five wins, and then graduated to Late Models in NASCAR's Weekly Racing Series in 1999, as he was turning 16.

In 2000 he joined the Hooter's ProCup Series, took rookie-of-the-year honors and became the youngest race winner in Series history.

Vickers was second in the ProCup points race in 2001, and also made four Busch Series starts. He drove a family-owned car during 21 Busch races in 2002 and when financing became tight Hendrick signed him for the following Busch season.

In 2003 Vickers won three Busch races and, at age 20, became the youngest national series champion in NASCAR history.

He also started five Cup races in 2003 and was promoted to the premier series full time in 2004, finishing 25th overall and winning his first two poles. He moved up to 17th in 2006 and finished second at Pocono after Carl Edwards passed him with 28 laps to go.

That was his career-best until he won at Talladega in his final six weeks with Hendricks. Toyota is banking on Vickers regaining the career momentum he lost in their first season together.

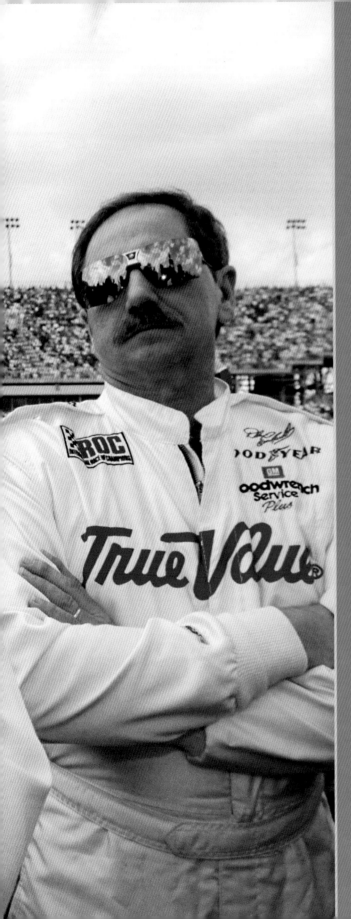

Taking a break from NASCAR Cup racing,
Dale Earnhardt Jr. and his father Dale
Earnhardt stand sentinel-like before the
start of an IROC race at Daytona in 1999.

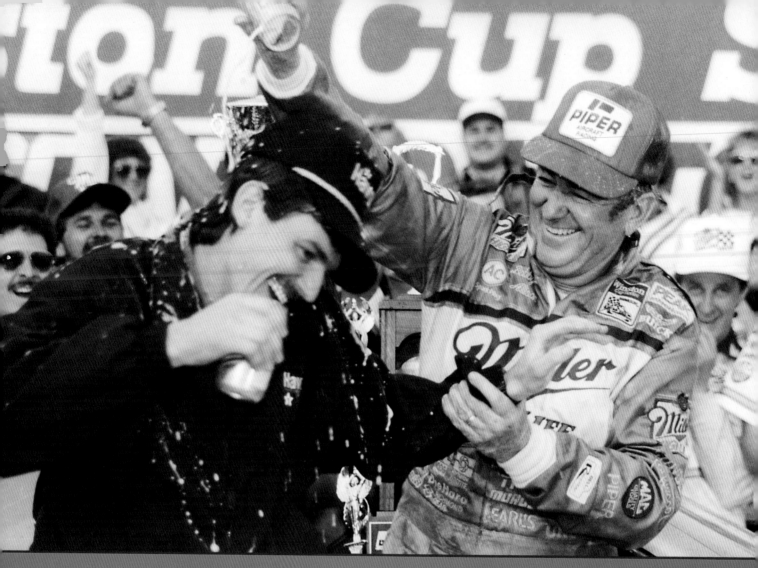

THE ALLISONS

The Allisons were on top after the 1988 Daytona 500. Bobby (right) picked up his third Daytona win, and son Davey took second place, a feat that has never been duplicated.

Tragedy seems to follow great racing families like a shadow, but few have been hit harder than the Allisons.

Brothers Bobby and Donnie Allison competed together at the lowest and highest levels of stock car racing throughout the 1950s, '60s, '70's and '80s, and Bobby's sons Davey and Clifford, set about doing the same thing. But in an unspeakably sorrowful 11-month period Clifford and Davey were both killed in accidents.

Clifford was fatally injured in mid-August, 1992, at Michigan International Speedway during practice for a Nationwide (then called Busch) Series race. He was only 27.

In July of 1993 Davey was piloting a helicopter he had purchased only three weeks earlier when it crashed at Talladega. He and family friend Red Farmer were traveling to see a practice run by David Bonnett, the son of another family friend, Neil Bonnett. Red survived the crash, but Davey died the next morning at the age of 32.

Davey had won 19 races in a Cup career that lasted only seven full seasons. When he arrived he was known as a quick racer with little patience. But when Larry McAllister became his crew chief at Robert Yates Racing in 1991, Davey calmed down and won 11 of his 19 victories.

When Davey was the 1987 rookie of the year, he became the first rookie to start in the front row of the Daytona 500 and the first rookie to win two races.

Driving for Robert Yates Racing, he almost won the 1992 points title, but lost it after a collision in the season finale.

By then, Donnie and Bobby had both been forced out of Cup racing by near-fatal accidents.

Donnie, who won 10 Cup races and 17 poles in a 22-year career in big-time stock car racing, suffered a serious accident during the 1981 World 600 and raced only 13 more times, the final race coming in 1988 at Michigan. Donnie was best known for his spectacular crossover weekend in 1970 when he finished fourth in the Indy 500, and then traveled to Charlotte and won the World 600.

Bobby's last race was also in 1988, at Pocono, where he sustained life-threatening head injuries that still affect his balance and memory.

It had been a happier time for the Allison family just a few months earlier when Bobby and Davey pulled off the unprecedented — and unequaled — father and son feat of finishing first and second in the Daytona 500. It was Bobby's third Daytona 500 title, and Davey would win the Great American Race four years later.

Both men called the 1988 Daytona 500 the greatest day of their racing lives, and both were selected among NASCAR's 50 greatest drivers of all time.

Bobby finished his career with 84 career Cup victories (tied for third all-time with Darrell Waltrip), one points title (1983) and as a six-time NASCAR Most Popular Driver. Hard-nosed on the track, he was the 1980 IROC champion and he won more than 600 short track races at several levels.

Bobby's success was all the more remarkable because he drove for several owners, including Bud Moore, Cotton Owens, Holman-Moody, Junior Johnson, Roger Penske and DiGard Racing.

He also piloted his own cars, including a Chevelle that brother Donnie built in their modest shop in 1966. Later that year Bobby raced the Chevelle to the first Allison career victory at Oxford, Maine.

Donnie and Bobby grew up in Miami and raced at Florida ovals in the late 1950s. But when they barnstormed Alabama and Bobby won bigger purses than he'd ever taken on his hometown tracks, he talked Donnie and their mentor, Red Farmer, into moving to Hueytown, Alabama, a stock-car hotbed. The trio, joined later by Neil Bonnett, were the founders of NASCAR's legendary "Alabama Gang."

The two brothers were part of one of the most publicized events in NASCAR history when Bobby came to Donnie's aid in a wild brawl with Cale Yarborough. It happened after

Yarborough and Donnie collided, allowing Richard Petty — with whom Bobby Allison had had a long feud — to win the 1979 Daytona 500. And it was all captured live on the first national television broadcast of the famous race.

After struggling through the death of their two sons — and Neil Bonnett's death in 1994 — Bobby Allison and his wife, Judy, divorced in 1996. Four years later they married each other again.

Grandson Robbie, 23 months old at the time of his father Davey's death, is now competing on amateur circuits in hopes of becoming the third-generation Allison to make Cup racing his career.

Another Daytona 500 victory pose, after Davey won the 1992 race. Mom Judy and Dad Bobby are the proud parents. Bobby stopped racing in 1988.

THE EARNHARDTS

An Earnhardt family portrait from 1986. Dale Sr. is all smiles after winning the Atlanta Journal 500, while wife Teresa and a young Dale Jr. look on during a happier moment in the family history.

Racing was one of the only roads out of the hard life at the cotton mill in Kannapolis, North Carolina. So Ralph Earnhardt took it.

His forays onto local dirt tracks in the early 1950s eventually led to a massive 21st-century Sprint Cup operation and both his son and grandson winning the Daytona 500.

Ralph didn't start racing until he was 25 and he made his name quickly. He won 32 races on the way to the NASCAR Sportsman title in 1956. During one portion of his career, he held the championship at seven different tracks.

Three generations of Earnhardts have now starred in NASCAR. The sport has rarely seen a more dominant presence than Ralph's son

Dale, who tied "King" Richard Petty's record of seven Cup titles, earning the nickname the "Terminator" in the process.

His son Dale Earnhardt Jr. continues the family tradition and is regularly voted the most popular driver on the Sprint Cup circuit. He captured the 2004 Daytona 500 on the sixth anniversary of his father's only victory in the sport's premier race.

Three years before Dale Jr.'s 500 win, Dale Sr. was killed on the final turn of the Great American Race, fully aware that his close friend Michael Waltrip had won his first Cup race in his 463rd attempt and that his son was the runner-up. Ralph, too, died with the sport: he was in his garage working on a car when he suffered a fatal heart attack in 1973, at the age of 45.

At the time of Dale Sr.'s tragic death, both his best friend and his son were racing under the colors of Dale Earnhardt Enterprises (DEI), which Dale Sr. and his wife, Teresa, founded in 1996 when Dale Jr. and his brother Kerry were developing in the sport.

Kerry worked at the family Chevrolet dealership before starting full time in racing. He won the 2000 ARCA RE/MAX Series, and that year competed against his father and brother in a Michigan Cup race. His sister Kelley also drove Late Model stocks, and most recently was Dale Jr.'s manager in the long, and ultimately fruitless, discussions to keep him in the family business.

After an acrimonious split from DEI in 2007, Dale Jr. moved over to Hendrick Motorsport, leaving behind his No. 8: a number that had become nearly as famous as his father's No. 3., which Dale Sr. made popular while driving for Richard Childress Racing, where he had won six of his seven Cup titles over a remarkable 17-year association with the team.

Dale Sr.'s path to the top started when he was 16, after dropping out of school in the ninth grade. He began racing for money shortly afterward and didn't make the Cup circuit for 12 more years — but once he got there he didn't waste any time moving to the top. Dale Sr. was rookie of the year in 1979 and he won his first Cup championship the following year.

There was something grand about Dale Sr.'s timing. On the same weekend that his father, Ralph, was inducted into the National Motorsports Press Association Hall of Fame in 1989, he won the Southern 500. And when both he and his father were selected among the 50 Greatest Drivers during NASCAR's 50th anniversary celebrations in 1998, Dale Sr. won his only Daytona 500.

Dale Jr. also knows how to seize a moment. In the second 2001 stop at Daytona, five months after his father had died there, he won the Pepsi 400 over Waltrip. It was a stirring and emotional victory for the young Earnhardt.

Like his father, Dale Jr. started professional racing at the age of 16. Within three years he was making his mark in the NASCAR Weekly Racing Series Late Model Division and over three seasons he finished in the top-10 in 90 of his 113 starts. He won the 1998 and 1999 Busch championships, and narrowly missed repeating his father's rookie-of-the-year Cup debut when he was second to freshman champ Matt Kenseth in 2000. Dale Jr. has yet to win his first points title, but entering 2008 he had 17 Cup victories and nearly $50 million in earnings.

There wasn't a dry eye at Daytona, or anywhere in the racing world, on February 2004 when he captured the 500.

"I don't know if I'll ever be able to tell this story and get it right," Dale Jr. said afterward. "My dad was in the passenger seat, having a ball."

His grandfather was probably there too.

Dale Sr. started his Cup driving career in 1979, won his first of seven championships the following season. The sport has never seen such a dominant figure, and may never again since his death in 2001.

THE FLOCKS

Tim Flock driving one of the potent Kiekhaefer Chryslers in 1956. He won a remarkable 18 races with the Chrysler in 1955.

In NASCAR's early years, there were a lot of charismatic drivers, but the Flock family retains a special place in the history of the sport.

Consisting of four brothers and two sisters, the Flock family moved to the Atlanta area from Alabama for better employment opportunities in the years before World War II.

Brothers Tim, Fonty and Bob learned their driving skills hauling moonshine around the back roads of Georgia. Carl raced boats. Sister Ethel, who also made her mark in racing, was named after the high-test gasoline of the time, and the youngest Flock, Reo (named after the car), took to sky-diving and wing-walking.

Born in 1924, Tim Flock, would have the most successful racing career in the family. He was on his way when he placed fifth at Charlotte in 1949 in NASCAR's new "Strictly Stock" division, a forerunner of today's Sprint Cup.

He was driving an Olds 88, one of the hottest cars at the time. Older brother Fonty took second in the race, driving a "Step-Down" Hudson. The following year, Tim won his first NASCAR race, the Grand National event at Charlotte.

Tim Flock was a dominant force in Grand National racing for the next several years, winning his first championship in 1952 behind the wheel of Ted Chester's Hudson, posting eight victories and 14 top-fives.

Tim said he wouldn't race NASCAR again after an altercation with NASCAR president Bill France in 1954, when France took away a victory for some illegal engine modifications. But in 1955, after Flock had opened and operated a Pure Oil station in Atlanta, friends convinced him to race Daytona.

Remarking that he could win the Daytona race if he had one of the new Chrysler 300s that were making waves, Flock found himself introduced to Carl Kiekhafer, the Mercury Outboard Motor president and the man behind the Chrysler assault on NASCAR.

As a result, Flock got into a Hemi-powered Chrysler and took the pole at Daytona Beach, finishing the race second behind Fireball Roberts (whose car was later deemed illegal). Tim would go on to win 18 of his 39 Grand National races and his second NASCAR championship in 1955, setting a NASCAR record that was not broken until Richard Petty won 19 races in 1967.

Tim Flock ran with Kiekhaefer and the Chryslers again in 1956, with three wins in his first eight races. But the spirited Flock was tired of the strict regimen of Kiekhaefer, and quit the team.

He continued to race, but never with the same success. In 1961 he again ran afoul of France when he tried to organize a drivers' union with fellow driver Curtis Turner. Both drivers were banned from NASCAR.

Although the ban was lifted in 1966, Flock had soured on driving. He did stay in racing, though, working as program director at the Charlotte Motor Speedway.

Tim Flock won 40 races and 37 pole positions in his 13-year NASCAR career. With the 40 victories coming in 189 starts, he holds a winning percentage of 21.2, the best in NASCAR NASCAR Grand National/Winston Cup history.

Tim Flock died in 1998, not before being inducted into the International Motorsports Press Hall of Fame in 1991 and the Stock Car Hall of Fame in 1995.

Old brother Fonty had a less successful career than Tim, but he was a force to be reckoned with in NASCAR's early days.

Running in semi-organized events prior to World War II, Fonty did well, but he was severely injured in a crash at Daytona in 1941, and he didn't return to racing until 1947.

In May of that year he won the inaugural stock car race at North Wilkesboro, and continued with victories at Charlotte, Trenton and Greensboro, winning the National Championship Stock Car Circuit (later named NASCAR).

In 1949 Fonty won NASCAR's Modified title with 11 victories, and then took to Grand National racing, finishing second in 1951, fourth in 1952, and fifth in 1953. He drove a limited schedule starting in 1954, and after a crash at Darlington in 1957, he parked it for good.

And sister Ethel was not just a flash-in-the-pan racer. Driving brother Fonty's Modified in the late 1940s, she raced in more than 100 events. Although she usually raced only in the Atlanta area, she did make a trip to Daytona in July of 1949, driving her 1949 Cadillac to an 11th-place finish, ahead of brothers Fonty and Bob. She also finished ahead of such early notables as Herb Thomas, Curtis Turner and Buck Baker.

Tim Flock with the victory spoils in 1957. The veteran won 40 NASCAR Grand National (now Sprint Cup) races in a career that spanned from 1949 to the early 1960s.

THE JARRETTS

Ned Jarrett not only started a family racing tradition; he started a broadcasting one too.

Known as "Gentleman Ned" for his calm demeanor and smooth interpersonal skills, Jarrett won 50 Cup races, and was followed into NASCAR by his son Dale, who retired five races into the 2008 season with 32 career victories.

Ned's other son, Glenn, had some Cup starts and was a regular in what is now the Nationwide Series. Daughter Patti also worked in racing, and grandson Jason earned some NASCAR starts and spotted for his father Dale's No. 44 Camry in his final full season.

Ned Jarrett was one of racing's broadcasting pioneers, starting with a regular weekly program on the radio station in his home town of Newton, North Carolina, while he was still racing in the early 1960s. In 1978 he started broadcasting on MRN radio, where he still has a regular show, and he later helped expand NASCAR's popularity as a TV commentator for CBS, ESPN and Fox Sports Network. Glenn now covers racing on cable TV.

Dale followed not only his father into auto racing, but into broadcasting, too, commentating with ESPN after his retirement.

One of the more indelible moments in Cup broadcast history came at the 1993 Daytona 500 when Dale won a bumper-to-bumper duel with Dale Earnhardt, with his father unabashedly urging him on from behind the CBS microphone. "They let my dad be a father instead of an announcer while calling that race, and it was special," Jarrett said at the 50th Daytona in 2008.

That was just the second win of Dale Jarrett's career, but he went on to win two more Daytona 500s and the 1999 Cup championship, as he and Ned became the second father and son combination (after Lee and Richard Petty) to win driver's titles.

Dale recalls being at the track as a six-year-old and watching his father run out of gas when he had a chance of winning the 1963 Daytona 500.

Ned won two driver's titles, in 1961 in his own car and in 1965, when he won 13 races for team owner Bondy Long, and finished in the top five in 42 of the 54 races. His win by 14 laps in that year's Southern 500 is still the largest margin of victory in Cup history.

Ned Jarrett became the only driver to retire as reigning Cup champion when he left the series after Ford announced during the 1966 season that it was withdrawing from NASCAR. He retired at only 34, while Dale was 41 when he finally hung up his fire suit.

Although Ned's 48 short-track victories are the third highest in Cup annals, he raced before the big money arrived, and his official career earnings were only $289,146. Dale Jarrett, among the best racers of his generation, left with nearly $60 million in Cup earnings.

The two generations had quite different racing origins too. Ned's father did not want him to compete in the dangerous sport, and his first few starts were under an assumed name.

Dale grew up around tracks but he was such a multi-talented athlete that it first seemed that he would accept a full golf scholarship at the University of North Carolina and turn professional in that sport. He was 20 before he chose racing, driving a car he and a couple of friends had put together for the Limited Sportsman division at hometown Hickory Motor Speedway.

Dale's Cup career started in 1984 and got off to a slow start. He didn't land his first win until 1991 at Michigan, when he gave the

Woods Brothers their first victory in 134 races. But from 1996 to 2001, he never finished the season out of the top five.

Dale has done his part to start some dynasties and traditions too. He was a charter member of the NASCAR Busch Series in 1982. He became Joe Gibbs Racing's inaugural driver in 1992, and he gave Gibbs his first Cup win with at the 1993 Daytona 500.

And when Michael Waltrip joined forces with Toyota for its first Cup season, Dale Jarrett moved over from Robert Yates Racing to be part of it. He was at the wheel of a Camry when he qualified for the 20th and last Daytona of his career in 2008, finishing 16th.

His father, of course, was there watching.

Dale Jarrett with the big check for winning the 1999 Cup championship. While Dale has won about $60 million racing, his father's official earnings are just shy of $290,000.

THE PETTYS

Only in this family could the "King" not be the head of the dynasty.

The Petty name is synonymous with stock car racing and no one has ever been more admired by NASCAR's legion of fans than Richard Petty. He was named NASCAR's most popular driver a stunning nine times and his fame transcended stock car's traditional sphere, earning him the nickname the "King."

But it was Richard's father, Lee Petty, who brought the family into NASCAR, where it has remained for four generations, one of the most prolific lineages in all of professional sport.

Petty Enterprises was founded by Lee in 1948 to be ready for NASCAR's inaugural Grand National (now Sprint Cup) Division in 1949.

When the company left its original home in Level Cross, North Carolina, prior to the 2008 season for more accessible quarters in Mooresville, it was as if baseball's Hall of Fame had left Cooperstown. Petty Enterprises, run by Richard and his son Kyle, who still drives in Sprint Cup, has been the home to 46 different Cup drivers, many of them all-time legends.

But it is the Petty name that carries the most clout.

Surprisingly, Lee Petty didn't begin racing until the advanced age of 35, when he climbed behind the wheel on the sands of Daytona Beach in 1949. But by the time he was done, his 54 wins were the career-high for any driver and he had become the first driver to win

Lee Petty, head of the Petty dynasty, is shown on the Daytona Beach in 1955 for a Modified race in his pre-war Ford coupe. He raced Plymouths and Oldsmobiles in NASCAR's early years, and perhaps his biggest victory came when he won the inaugural Daytona 500 in 1959.

three points titles (1954, 1958 and 1959).

When the Daytona 500 made its debut in 1959, Lee was one of the doubters and admitted to being fearful of its high steep banks. Nevertheless, he competed in the debut race and won a three-across photo finish with Joe Weatherly and Johnny Beauchamp, although it took three days for Petty to be declared the champion.

As Lee Petty drove the No. 42 to the first Daytona win, his son Richard was struggling in the No. 43, and managed to complete only eight laps. But Richard would go on to win an unprecedented and unmatched seven Daytona 500s, including his first one in 1964, the year his father retired from racing.

Richard's record seven Cup titles were later matched by Dale Earnhardt, but nobody has come close to what he did in 1967. The King won 27 times, including 10 in a row, and finished among the top five in 38 of the 48 official races. It is considered the greatest single season in racing history.

Richard broke Lee's record on the way to the all-time high of 200 Cup victories and also holds career marks in poles (127) and starts (1,177).

Richard Petty continued racing until 1992, when he retired at the age of 55. He's still a fixture at the track and, as always, makes time for his myriad fans. Arguably, the King has done more than anyone else to spread the NASCAR gospel.

"My daddy was a race driver, so I became a race driver," he says. "I grew up around race cars. I've been working on 'em since I was 12. It's all I know, really."

While Richard went behind the wheel of the family business, his brother Maurice went under the hood and became the company's engine builder. Maurice's son Tim began building the Petty Enterprise power plants in 1982.

Richard's son Kyle is a multi-talented man who runs marathons, was offered a baseball scholarship and had a chance to become a country singer.

Like his father and grandfather, though, Kyle concentrated on racing and was third in the 1980 Cup rookie-of-the-year standings. He left the family firm, gaining experience over four years with the Woods Brothers and another eight with Felix Sabates. He also picked up eight Cup wins.

Kyle returned to Petty Enterprises in 1997 and now runs the day-to-day business operation as well as driving one of the team's two Cup cars. Bobby Labonte races in Richard's famous No. 43, while Kyle drives No. 45 in honor of his late son, Adam.

Adam Petty, the fourth generation of the racing Pettys, was killed during a Busch race practice at New Hampshire in May of 2000. Adam, only 19, had made his Cup debut a few weeks earlier, just three days before Lee Petty died at the age of 86.

A 22-year-old Richard with his somewhat tattered number 43 Oldsmobile convertible in 1959. His number would become the most famous ever painted on a race car.

THE WALTRIPS

There's a huge gap in their ages and an even bigger difference in their NASCAR careers, but Darrell and Michael Waltrip have a lot in common.

It starts with the family name of course, and their grounding in Owensboro, Kentucky, where Darrell was born in 1947 and Michael arrived in 1963. That background has given each of the brothers a drawling charisma that drips of stock car racing's origins.

While Michael's easy warmth and million-dollar smile won him quick success with fans and the sponsorship world, Darrell's outspoken nature made him public enemy No. 1 early in his career.

But Darrell's continued witicisms and success—three-times Cup champion, three times runner-up — chipped away at racing fans' resentment and he was eventually voted NASCAR's most popular driver in 1989 and 1990. Instead of his original nickname of "Jaws," given him by Cale Yarborough, he's now known as "Ole D.W."

Both Waltrips are leading broadcasters: Darrell does TV race-day analysis, with a signature "boogity, boogity, boogity" count-down to the green flag; Michael regularly works on speciality TV channels and radio.

Beginning in 1972, Darrell was a Cup racer for 28 seasons. In 2008 Michael entered his 23rd full-time Cup season.

Both brothers became driver owners, and each gambled on Toyota's interest — Darrell in 2004 with his Craftsman Truck team and Michael as a driver and owner with Toyota's graduation into Sprint Cup racing in 2007.

Each Waltrip befriended Dale Earnhardt, Darrell's onetime arch-rival on and off the track, and drove for the company the Terminator owned, Dale Earnhardt Enterprises (DEI). Darrell raced briefly for DEI late in his career, and Michael spent five years there before an unhappy parting in 2006.

Among all this, however, the Waltrips will be forever linked by the Daytona 500, the only event in which the younger brother outshone the older.

Darrell had won the 1981, 1982 and 1985 points titles for legendary Junior Johnson, and was the dominant Cup driver from 1979 to 1986. Despite this success, the Great American Race confounded Darrell almost as much as it did his pal Earnhardt (who took his victory lap in 1998). Darrell finally won in 1989 in his 17th try, and his post-race cry, "I ain't dreamin' am I?" is part of 500 lore.

Michael also broke a dramatic drought by winning the Daytona 500 in 2001. It was his first start in a DEI car, and his first career Cup win, after 461 previous starts.

And it was Darrell's first broadcast for Fox Sports. He abandoned all objectivity and urged his brother across the line, yelling, "You got it, you got it, you got it. Mikeeeyyyy!"

The brothers' shared joy turned to sorrow a few minutes later when Dale Earnhardt died from the injuries he suffered on the final turn. Darrell became a forceful and ultimately successful advocate for head-and-neck restraints.

Michael went on to win the Daytona 500 again in 2003, and his only other two career victories have also been in restrictor plate races, at Talladega in 2003 and in Daytona's 2002 summer race.

In Michael's debut Cup race, at Charlotte in 1985, Darrell won. Michael has never finished higher than 12th in the points standings, but is one of the most engaging drivers on the circuit. Since 1996 he has owned a strong Nationwide Series team — David Reutimann was runner-up in 2007 — and in 2007 he joined with Toyota to run three Cup cars.

Darrell has been a far more successful driver and broadcaster than owner, and had to fold his own Cup team in the late 1990s. He returned in 2004 to join Toyota in Craftsman Trucks.

But he was easily selected as one of the NASCAR's top 50 drivers of all time. His 84 career Cup wins are tied with Bobby Allison for third place overall, and his 59 poles rank fourth all-time. Although he raced seven more seasons after his final Cup win in 1992, he still won at the astounding rate of every 9.6 starts in his career. And his switch to Tide in 1987 significantly broadened the scope of NASCAR sponsorship.

There is also no doubt that he blazed a trail for his younger brother.

"I've always raced because that's what I wanted to do," Michael says. " But when I was a kid growing up in Kentucky, no one else's brother was off racing against Richard Petty."

Darrell Waltrip (right) was still a major player in 1985 when younger brother Michael (left) followed Darrell into NASCAR. Here, a pensive Harry Gant is surrounded by the brothers in 1991 at Charlotte before the Coca-Cola 600.

THE WOODS

By 1971, when this picture was taken at Daytona, the Wood Brothers were masters at the speedy and efficient pit stop. Here the team is filling David Pearson's Mercury.

Glen Wood was named one of the top 50 drivers in NASCAR history, but really made his name from being behind cars rather than inside them.

Wood Brothers Racing, which Glen founded in 1950 when he began competing regularly, has been a family affair from the start. And not just the Wood family. Edsel Ford, the great-grandson of Henry Ford, once said he considers the Woods part of the Ford family, because they've run the giant automaker's cars since the company began.

Glen Wood first climbed into a stock car at a track near Martinsville, Virginia, and wrecked in his debut race. As he was towing the damaged car home, it burst into flames and burned to a crisp. Undaunted by what might have been a bad omen, he moved up to compete on the emerging NASCAR circuit. Glen won four premier series races before leaving the cockpit for good in 1964 to become a full-time owner. He had already become crew chief for the team's other drivers in 1961, with his younger brother, Leonard, as his assistant.

Leonard was with the team from the beginning, building the engines and perfecting the rapid pit stops for which the company became renowned. He is regarded as the forefather of the modern pit stop, which helped such drivers as Cale Yarborough, Tiny Lund and Fireball Roberts become legends.

Not restricting themselves to stock cars, the brothers pit-crewed Jimmy Clark to victory in the 1965 Indy 500. Their biggest Cup successes came with David Pearson, who won 11 races in 1973 and another 10 in 1976.

Donnie Allison, Dale Jarrett, Neil Bonnett, Ricky Rudd and Ken Schrader have all raced for the Woods. And when NASCAR selected its top 50 drivers in 1998, a whopping 17 of them had driven a Wood Brothers car at some point in their careers.

When Glen Wood retired from day-to-day operations in the late 1980s, his sons Eddie and Len took over the business and his daughter, Kim, continued to work with her mother on all the administrative details of the company.

Len has become the engine specialist and Eddie works on the marketing end of the business, keeping the famous No. 21 car financed with sponsorships.

As the business of Cup racing became increasingly sophisticated and demanding, in 2003 the Woods finally moved out of their modest headquarters in Stuart, Virginia, where the family business had operated for its first 53 years.

After two years in Mooresville, North Carolina, the team moved to its current facility in Harrisburg, North Carolina, not far from Lowe's Motorspeedway.

In order to compete against the multi-car teams, Wood Brothers and JTG Racing joined forces for 2006 and 2007, but split back into separate competition components before the 2008 season. They still work together in marketing and a few other areas, and share shop space.

The Woods have won 96 Cup races and finished in the top five 336 times, but victories have been scarce in recent years. Heading into the 2008 season, the company's last win in NASCAR's top circuit was Elliott Sadler's victory at Bristol in 2001.

And when Bill Elliott couldn't qualify the car for the 2008 Daytona 500, it was only the third time in the history of stock car's greatest race, and first since 1962, that the Woods hadn't had a car on the starting grid.

"It's hard to compete when you're running with one car," Eddie Woods said.

As well as the No. 21 Sprint Cup car, the Woods also own the No. 21 in the Craftsman Truck Series. Eddie's son Jon Wood and his

cousin Keven Wood, Len's son, share the truck ride, and Keven continues to race on Viriginia and North Carolina ovals.

Jon also has a selected number of Sprint Cup starts.

During Daytona testing in 2008, the young cousins continued the family tradition. Keven was in the control tower spotting for Jon.

"I'm looking forward to Jon and I sharing the driving duties of the truck," Keven said. "We always figured it would happen some day.

"I know I don't have to go far for advice, if I need it. I know Jon will be right there for me, along with my dad and Uncle Eddie, both in the pits."

Where the family has always been.

The Woods also fielded cars driven by others, such as Cale Yarborough (right), here celebrating his 1967 Atlanta 500 win with Delano Wood (left) and Glen Wood.

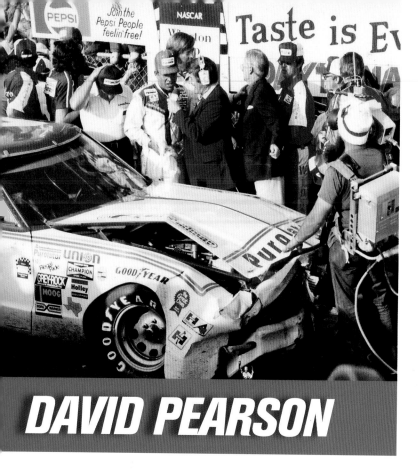

DAVID PEARSON

Pearson, with his smashed-up Mercury, explains his last-lap crash with Richard Petty, which allowed him to win the 1976 Daytona 500, to a television crew.

One of the great stock car drivers, David Pearson amassed 105 NASCAR Cup victories, second only to all-time leader Richard Petty, with 200 wins.

Many speculate if he had raced as long as Petty he would have taken the "King of Stock Car Racing" title. A South Carolina native born in 1934, Pearson was NASCAR champ three times and leads the all-time win ratio with 18 percent. As a sample of this strength, he won 11 of the 18 races he entered in 1973.

Pearson started his racing career on dirt tracks in 1952. By 1960 he was on the NASCAR circuit, and took 18th at Daytona. The next year not only did he win his first Grand National (today's Sprint Cup) race, and capture the World 600, the Firecracker 250, and the Dixie 400 at Atlanta but he was the first driver to accomplish this in a single year. And he won the 1961 rookie-of-the-year honors.

Throughout the 1960s Pearson was dominant in NASCAR's top class, first in Dodges, and then in the familiar number 21 Mercury and Ford Talladega mounts.

Pearson's physical attributes played a large part in his success. In the 1960s it took muscle to handle cars in those long races with no power steering, and his stout stature served him well.

In 1964 he won eight events on the short tracks, and two years later won 10 of 15 races on dirt tracks and enough events on the rest of the circuit to give him his first NASCAR championship.

By the end of the decade, Pearson's late-race, pedal-to-the-floor style had taken hold, and in 1968 and 1969 he won top honors again, acquiring the nickname "The Silver Fox" for his driving prowess. He was a master at playing his cards close to the vest. When running well, he would lurk a few positions back from the leader, and then turn it up a few notches to take the lead on the last lap.

In this heady time in NASCAR history, the late-race duels between Pearson and Petty offered some of the most exciting and memorable finishes in NASCAR racing. This high-profile duo finished one–two 63 times, Pearson taking 33 of those victories.

One of their most famous finishes occurred at the end of the 1976 Daytona 500, a race Pearson had never won in 17 attempts.

As Pearson and Petty entered the last lap on the 2.5-mile oval, Petty led and all waited for Pearson to make his move. Going into turn three, Pearson took the lead but drifted high near the wall, and Petty regained the lead by a couple of feet. The two tangled in turn four, with Pearson going into the wall and Petty sliding down into the infield. The King was 50 yards away from winning with a car he couldn't get started. With no other cars on the lead lap, Pearson kept his Mercury running and limped across the line to win his first Daytona 500.

Although Pearson never suffered any race-related injuries in his career, with failing eyesight and persistent back problems, he retired from driving in 1986 at age 52.

GLENN 'FIREBALL' ROBERTS

Fireball is all smiles with the race queens after capturing the 1962 Daytona 500 with one of Smokey Yunick's powerhouse Pontiacs.

A master of the super speedways, Edward Glenn "Fireball" Roberts has been called one of NASCAR's greatest drivers, and his persona dominated stock car racing in the late 1950s and early 1960s. He was a superstar before the name had been coined. While his star did not burn long, it burned brighter than that of any other driver.

Born in Daytona Beach, Florida, in 1931, Roberts got his nickname for his pitching ability in high school baseball, and although he attended the University of Florida for a while, his heart was telling him to go racing.

After a so-so racing career starting with NASCAR in 1949, Roberts divided his racing between the Grand National and Modified divisions in the 1950s, and in 1956 won five GN events.

In 1959 a new era of stock car racing began with the opening of the super speedways, tracks such as Daytona, paved ovals of two miles or more in length, where drivers could attain new benchmarks of speed.

Also in 1959, Roberts began his relationship with legendary race car builder Henry

"Smokey" Yunick, and this combination was a tough one to beat for the next several years as Roberts' racing career took off, driving those black and gold Pontiacs of Yunick. He was calculating, crafty and knowledgeable, and was the best at the "sling shot" pass, now part of "drafting."

Running 30 super speedway races from 1959 to 1962, Roberts won five of them, and put the Pontiac on the pole in fifteen. His favorite playground was Daytona, where he won so often that fans started calling the track "Fireball International Raceway."

By the time Roberts was 30 years old, the sport was starting to wear on him. His passion was not what it once was, and he was not as dominant. By 1964 he would spin out on tracks that he had previously mastered. He admitted to friends he wanted out, maybe try his hand at broadcasting. He also mentioned getting out entirely and buying a beer distributorship.

But he was contractually bound to race for the Ford team of Holman-Moody and the sponsors. In May of 1964 he headed to Charlotte and the World 600, which would be his last race.

Prophetically, Fireball's car hit the wall and burst into flames after getting into a smash-up with Junior Johnson and Ned Jarrett. With Jarrett's help, Roberts was able to get out of the burning Ford, but he suffered burns to 75 percent of his body. He held on in hospital, but died six weeks later, at the age of 34.

During his career, Roberts won 32 Grand National races, including four victories at Daytona, and set more than 400 NASCAR records. He was inducted into the International Motorsports Hall of Fame in 1990, and the Stock Car Hall Fame in 1993.

MARSHALL TEAGUE

One of NASCAR's pioneers, Teague understood promoting himself long before others, and his alliance with Hudson in the early years gave the team many victories.

Marshall Teague was one of NASCAR's pioneer drivers, and one of the first in the new sport to realize the power of promotion.

Born in 1922, this Daytona Beach garage owner won seven of 23 races entered from 1951 to 1953, driving his famed Hudson Hornet. Teague realized the potential of the Hudson of that era, which featured superior handling characteristics over Oldsmobiles and Plymouths. He went to the Hudson factory in Detroit and left the carmaker's offices as the first driver to obtain factory support from the car-maker, which supplied him with "export" options such as heavy-duty suspension and engine parts.

Along with Hudson, Teague acquired the sponsorship of the Pure Oil Company. And he also acquired the services of the legendary Smokey Yunick as engine builder and crew chief for his Hudson.

Known as "The King of the Beach" for his victories on the early Daytona beach-road course, Teague won five Grand National races in the 1951 season in only 15 starts. He took second to Robert "Red" Byron in the first-ever NASCAR-sanctioned race, a Modified event held on the Daytona beach-road course in February of 1948.

Traveling in the early 1950s was an arduous task. Most of the time the race car was flat-towed behind the street car, on narrow two-lane highways, as the Interstate highway system was just getting started. Teague didn't mind, and he set his sights farther west.

Teague won the first NASCAR Cup race west of the Mississippi River, taking the victory in the Gardena 200-lapper on the half-mile Carrell Speedway dirt track in April of 1951. He repeated his performance on a large mile dirt track at the Arizona State Fairgrounds in Phoenix, also in April of 1951. On lap 81 of the 150-lap contest, Teague took the lead from Fonty Flock in an Oldsmobile. Teague pocketed $2,500 for his two race victories.

In 1953 Teague began racing in the stock car ranks of the American Automobile Association and the U.S Auto Club circuits. NASCAR founder Bill France did not appreciate Teague racing for rival sanctioning bodies, so Teague left NASCAR.

Teague's AAA and USAC career was somewhat spotty over the next few years. He won two AAA Stock Car titles, in 1952 and 1954, and placed seventh in the Indy 500 in 1957, but his victories were not nearly as common as in his early NASCAR days. So Teague returned to his NASCAR roots in 1959. And it wasn't to race stock cars.

France had just finished building the first super speedway, the Daytona International Speedway, a two and a half-mile oval that has become world famous. To promote this new paved facility back in 1959, France posted a $10,000 prize for the first driver to reach 160 mph.

Driving a special, home-built, open-wheeled Indy-style car, Teague took to the new tri-oval on February 11, 1959. But aerodynamics and wind-tunnel testing were not yet part of auto racing. Teague's car got out of control, flipped over and killed him. He was 36.

CURTIS TURNER

Turner was perhaps the best natural driver in NASCAR, especially on the dirt tracks. He was also a master in NASCAR's convertible division, and is shown here in his favorite 1956 Ford at Winston-Salem in NC. He won 22 times with this car in 1956.

Curtis Turner was the poster boy of stock car racing in the early years.
This hard-driving, hard-working, and hard-drinking Virginian lived life the way he wanted and was the most colorful personality on a race track in the 1950s and 1960s.

Turner was a master behind the wheel, amassing wins in NASCAR and ARCA, and at Pike's Peak. But he was hard on his cars, and not above running others off the track to win a race.

Nicknamed "Pops" for "popping" slower cars out of his way, Turner would settle his differences with other drivers both on and off the track. Some of his encounters with fellow competitor Lee Petty have become legendary. He was the original "Intimidator" long before Dale Earnhardt earned that name, and Turner would make today's NASCAR drivers look like altar boys.

Born in the Blue Ridge Mountains of Virginia in 1924, Turner won his first race in 1949 on the Langhorne, PA, dirt oval in an Oldsmobile. This was the first of over 350 wins, including 18 NASCAR Grand Nationals and 38 NASCAR Convertible division victories.

Turner holds several distinctions. For one, he is the only driver to win two Grand National races in a row from the pole by leading every lap, which happened in Rochester, NY, and Charlotte, NC, in 1950.

And he is the only driver to win 25 major NASCAR events in one season driving the same car. In 1956 Turner took 22 wins in a Ford convertible, and then won three more races, including the Southern 500, in the same car with the top welded on, a common practice at the time.

Turner later became the first to qualify for a Grand National race at a speed greater than 180 mph, accomplished at the 1967 Daytona 500 in a "Smokey" Yunick Chevrolet.

Turner's business career was not as successful as his racing. While his main business concern was in the lumber industry, he was the man behind the Charlotte Motor Speedway. The concept, financing and construction were his, but when this new speedplant opened in 1960, there were serious money problems.

Turner did everything possible to get the track's financing in order, including a great deal of personal investing, but he was out of his league, and the track's board of directors ousted him as president in 1961.

Later that year Turner tried to organize NASCAR drivers as a union entity. NASCAR president Bill France put a stop to that, and gave Turner a lifetime suspension.

France and Turner made up in 1965, and Turner returned to plying his trade in Grand National events, but he came less frequently to the tracks. NASCAR was becoming a professional sport with a national presence, and there was no room in it for the antics that made Turner famous.

Turner was a skilled pilot. He flew frequently on business matters with no incidents, but in October, 1970, he crashed his plane with golfer Clarence King in Pennsylvania. There were no survivors. Turner was 46.

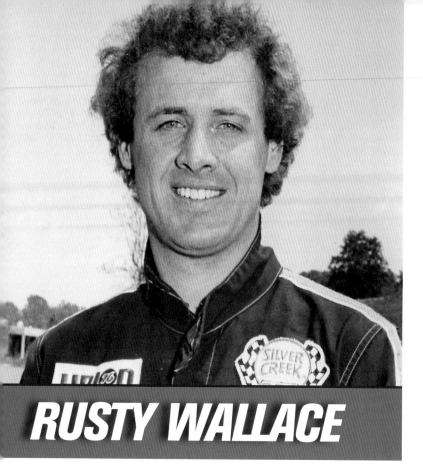

RUSTY WALLACE

A Missouri native who thrived on the bullrings of the Midwest before heading south, Wallace is shown here in his ASA days. He won 55 Cup events, and is now a television commentator for the sport.

When Rusty Wallace finished third in his final race at Dover International Speedway, there was a sense he might do the impossible ... win the Nextel Cup in his final racing year.

With that top-five at Dover, Wallace moved into second place in the Nextel Cup points standings with eight races still remaining in the 2005 Chase. Since he'd announced his retirement and promoted the season as "Rusty's Last Call," the game caught the public's attention. Wallace eventually finished eighth overall, and stepped out of the familiar Penske No. 2 Dodge with his head held high.

The charismatic Wallace left Cup racing with 706 starts, the 1989 Winston Cup championship, the eighth-highest win total in history (55), and a stunning top-10 total of 349.

Wallace's on-track legacy includes a streak of 10 years among the elite 10 in the points standing. When he finished 14th in 2004 and 16th the next year, it seemed that his run near the top was done. But then he returned with that improbable farewell season.

The final victory of his magnificent career was Martinsville, the eighth race of 2004.

"It's an honor to be compared to those guys such as Petty, Allison or Pearson," Wallace said. "I questioned a lot of things during that [two year] dry spell." Dry spells were rare for Wallace.

The oldest of three brothers who all graduated to Cup driving, Wallace gravitated to the sport early from their Missouri home. Wallace was the Central Racing Association's rookie of the year in 1973 and won more than 200 stock car races before joining the USAC circuit in 1979. In that fabulous debut year, he won five races and was second in points standings.

Roger Penske gave him a couple of Winston Cup rides in 1980, and Wallace made the most of the chance, finishing second to the late Dale Earnhardt in his debut in Atlanta. After seven more Cup races over the next two years, he won the 1983 ASA championship and joined NASCAR Cup racing full time in 1984, driving for Cliff Stewart. His 14th-place finish as a rookie started a string of 22 seasons in the top 20.

He joined Raymond Beadle in 1986 and won his first race, at Bristol, his favorite track. When he won six times in 1988 and was runner-up to series champion Bill Elliott by just 24 points, NASCAR observers recognized a future Cup champion.

The future arrived only a year later, when Wallace again won six races and edged Earnhardt by 12 points for the 1989 Winston Cup championship.

In 1991 Wallace jumped to Penske as driver and co-owner of the Miller Genuine Draft Pontiac. After a down year in 1992, he rebounded in 1993, with a career-high 10 victories, and finished second in the points championship.

Over the next nine years he finished third, fifth, fourth, eighth, ninth and seventh (four times) before dropping to 14th in 2001. After the Martinsville win in 2004 and his 2005 farewell tour, he walked right into the broadcast booth and into the Hall of Fame.

HENRY 'SMOKEY' YUNICK

Smokey is shown here behind Bobby Unser who is climbing into a Camaro road course car for the 1969 Paul Revere 250 at Daytona. Yunick was a mechanical genius who applied his talents not only to auto racing but also to the internal combustion engine, and the fields of aviation and oil. Some of his inventions rest in the Smithsonian.

In a sport filled with colorful characters in its early years, none was as colorful as Henry "Smokey" Yunick.

Not only was Yunick a master mechanic who fielded a massive quantity of race cars, but he brought his technological improvements to the auto racing world, and his reputation as a mechanical genius continues to this day.

From "The Best Damn Garage in Town," his shop in Daytona Beach, Yunick became the most innovative and influential crew chief/ mechanic in NASCAR history. His cars won over 50 races, and he was associated with more than 50 of the most prominent drivers in U.S. racing.

Yunick's most legendary achievement was his ability to circumvent standard racing rules and technology. He didn't bend the rules, he massaged them. His creative juices worked at a whole other level than those of his contemporaries.

Born in 1923 and raised on a Pennsylvania farm, Yunick started his mechanical creativity with tractors. While he was competing in a motorcycle race in 1941, the announcer forgot his name, but Yunick's bike was smoking a lot, so he acquired the nickname "Smokey."

After serving as a B-17 bomber pilot in World War II, Yunick set up shop in Daytona Beach in 1946 and started building Hudson Hornet engines for NASCAR pioneer driver Herb Thomas. In the mid-50s he turned to Chevrolet, then Ford, switching over to Pontiac with drivers Fireball Roberts, Paul Goldsmith and Marvin Panch. His cars won four of the first eight major races at Daytona through to 1962.

On the NASCAR scene, Yunick switched back to Chevrolet in 1963 and helped develop the new big-block 427-cubic-inch engine for the GM division. Although Chevy was officially out of NASCAR racing, Yunick continued working with Chevy in a semi-secret fashion, fielding a series of Chevelle-based cars as an independent.

During this time, prodded by the factory-based Chrysler and Ford teams, NASCAR paid much closer attention to Yunick's winning cars, and he and the tech inspectors had a lot of tussles over rule interpretation.

He left NASCAR in 1970, after winning 57 Cup races. He worked on Indy cars for a few years but then quit racing to continue his inventions and work on conservation issues. He also kept an interest in aviation, continued his truck dealership and developed more functional oil field machinery.

Yunick was a technical advisor and personal consultant to many automobile, automobile-related, and oil companies. He wrote several books and for 30 years was on the staff of several auto magazines. His inventions, some of which are in the Smithsonian Institution, include variable ratio power steering, extended tip spark plugs, race track crash barriers, and hot vapor engines. He continued efforts to build a better mousetrap until his death in May, 2001.

The list of Yunick's drivers reads like a Who's Who of U.S. racing. NASCAR drivers include Bobby Allison, Paul Goldsmith, Tim and Fonty Flock, Curtis Turner, "Fireball" Roberts, Ralph Moody, Buck Baker and Cotton Owens. Indy car drivers include Al and Bobby Unser, Mario Andretti, A.J. Foyt, Joe Leonard, Gordon Johncock and Tony Bettenhausen.

NASCAR HALL OF FAME — CHARLOTTE

The long-awaited NASCAR Hall of Fame and Museum is scheduled to open in 2010 in Charlotte, North Carolina, and will showcase all aspects of the sport, including its rich history.

When the NASCAR Hall of Fame opens early in 2010, Buz McKim will be ready.

As the Hall of Fame's historian, McKim has been collecting materials for the new 130,000 square foot facility in Charlotte, North Carolina. He spends a great deal of time traveling, but not just to collect programs and souvenirs and photos. He also checks out race cars from the past to ensure their authenticity for placement in the new building.

There will be 50,000 square feet of exhibit space showcasing the history and heritage of the sport, and McKim plans to cover as much of this as possible.

"We're going to tell the whole story," says McKim. "We're going right back before NASCAR was born. There are a ton of things we want to do, and this is a chance to tell it all."

There will be exhibits for every facet of NASCAR, including involvement in drag racing, the Daytona Beach speed trials and its Speedway Division.

The Hall of Fame will also include a 250-seat theater, a Hall of Honor for inductees, and racing simulators. In addition, the Hall will feature 15 to 20 historic race cars, a full-size race transporter, and many individual galleries depicting the sphere of NASCAR.

"Everything will be significant," McKim went on to say. "We know what's there and how to get it. We also know what is real and what's bologna. We've been doing our homework."

an original 1986 Dale Earnhardt car, there are memorabilia, photos, and all six Winston Cup banners and trophies won by RCR.

Roush Fenway Racing Museum

The Roush Fenway facility includes the team's first Cup win car, Mark Martin's Thunderbird, the Cup cars of Matt Kenseth and Greg Biffle, and cars from Roush's other racing, including drag racing and Trans Am racing.

Hendrick Motorsports

Some of Jeff Gordon's winning cars are housed here in a 15,000 square foot area of the shop, plus a Cup car in various stages of build. Hendrick also has on display Terry Labonte's "Iron Man" Monte Carlo, the car he drove to tie Richard Petty's career-record 513 starts.

Penske

The Penske facility is huge, at over 424,000 square feet, and close to half of this area is for its NASCAR shop, where there is provision for visitors to watch employees work on Cup cars. The building also houses cars and work areas for Penske's Indy car and ALMS racing.

Yates

Robert Yates Racing has a museum in its building with several race cars and pieces of memorabilia, plus an area to watch cars under construction.

Gillett Evernham

Although there isn't a lot of history in the shop of one of the newer NASCAR teams, visitors can watch car building in progress and see Bill Elliott's Daytona 500 pole-winning Dodge Intrepid.

Several present and former Cup drivers have their own museums and displays, including Mark Martin, Richard Petty and Joe Weatherly. Recently, Tony Stewart had cars from his illustrious career on display in the Indianapolis Speedway Museum.

Museums and Race Car Shops

There are a number of auto racing museums that display NASCAR cars and exhibits, right from its earliest years. Several NASCAR Cup teams in the Charlotte, North Carolina, area have exhibits from their past in their racing shops, along with present car and shop displays that offer a great deal of insight and history into the sport. Here are some examples.

RCR Racing Museum

The Richard Childress Racing shop and museum of 47,000 square feet holds over 40 race cars from its 35-year career. Along with

GLOSSARY

ACT American-Canadian Tour

Aerodynamics The science of understanding different forces acting on a moving element in gases such as air. As applied to racing, the study of airflow and the forces of resistance and pressure that result from the flow of air over, under and around a moving car. The application of this study to racing is credited with much of the sport's recent progress as teams learn more about drag, air turbulence and downforce.

Air dam The front valance of the vehicle, which produces downforce while directing air flow around the car.

ALMS American Le Mans Series

Anti-roll bars Bars running in the front of the car, which help control how much the car tips from side to side; linking suspension parts which can be adjusted to alter handling characteristics to compensate for tire wear and varying fuel loads.

Apron The paved portion of a racetrack which separates the racing surface from the (usually unpaved) infield. The very bottom of the racetrack, below the bottom groove. If a car has a problem, the driver goes there to get out of the way.

ARCA Automobile Racing Club of America

ASA American Speed Association

Back stretch The straight on a circle track between turns two and three.

Backup car A secondary complete and set-up stock car brought to NASCAR races by each team, transported and stored in the front half of the upper level of team haulers. Backup cars must pass all NASCAR inspections. The backup car may not be unloaded at any time during all NASCAR National Series practice or pre-race competition activities unless the primary car is damaged beyond repair.

Balance A term that aero engineers use to describe downforce, front to rear. Balance is also used to explain the situation when, in a perfect world, the least amount of drag is produced for the most downforce exerted.

Banking The sloping of a racetrack, particularly at a curve or corner, from the apron to the outside wall. "Degree of banking" refers to the height of a track's slope at its outside edge.

Black box Unlike airplane black boxes, which store recording devices, a race car's black box contains high-tech electrical systems that control most engine functions. More technically referred to as the "engine electronic controls," the "engine control unit" or the "engine management system."

Blister Excessive heat can make a tire literally blister and shed rubber. Drivers can detect the problem by the resulting vibrations, and risk more serious damage if they choose not to pit.

Blocking Changing position on the track to prevent drivers behind from passing. Blocking is accepted if a car is defending position in the running order, but considered unsportsmanlike if lapped cars hold up more competitive teams.

Brake scoop Openings in the body panel and other locations of a stock car which take in air for cooling. A maximum of three scoops per brake is permitted by NASCAR officials, with a maximum of three-inch flexible hose to the brake.

Bump drafting A version of drafting in which one car bumps another. The initial contact breaks downforce and drag forces momentarily, giving the lead car as much as 100 more usable horsepower, rocketing it away from the pack without totally breaking the draft.

Camber The angle that wheels are tilted inward or outward (the angle that a tire seizes to the track surface) from vertical. If the top of the wheel is tilted inward, the camber is negative.

Caster The angle of a spindle frontward or rearward. "Caster stagger" is the difference between the static caster settings; it affects the amount of pull to the right or left a driver experiences. The more caster stagger, the more the vehicle pulls or steers.

CART Championship Auto Racing Teams

Chassis The basic structure of a race car to which all other components are attached. CART cars have carbon-fiber monocoque tubes, while a NASCAR stock car has a steel tube frame chassis.

Chute A racetrack straightaway, either on an oval or a road course.

Circulating Driving around a track with a damaged and/or slow car to accumulate laps and, more importantly, points and prize money.

Combinations Combinations of engine, gearing, suspension, aerodynamic parts, and wheel and tire settings which teams forecast will work under varying conditions and tracks. These combinations (also known as set-ups) are recorded and used as a baseline when teams arrive at a track.

Compound The rubber blend for tires. In some series, teams can choose their tire compound based on the track and weather conditions. A softer compound tire provides better traction but wears out much faster than a harder compound tire, which doesn't provide as much grip. Different tracks require different tire compounds. Left-side tires are considerably softer than right-side tires and it's against the rules to run left sides on the right.

Dialed in A car that is handling very well. The car isn't loose or tight; it's comfortable to the driver's liking.

Dirty air Turbulent air caused by fast-moving cars, which can cause a particular car to lose control. "I got in his air."

DNF Did not finish.

DNQ Did not qualify.

DNS Did not start.

Downforce The downward pressure of the air on a car as it races. Downforce increases with velocity, or the rapidity of motion or speed. It is determined by such things as front fenders and rear spoilers.

Draft Airflow creates a low-pressure air pocket (or draft) behind moving objects. Most notably in NASCAR, drivers try to follow opponents closely enough to enter their draft and benefit from a towing effect. The car creating the draft actually pulls the pursuing driver, who can ease off the throttle and save gas.

Drafting Practice of two or more cars to run nose to tail while racing, almost touching. The lead car, by displacing air in front of it, creates a vacuum between its rear end and the following car's nose.

Duct work The enclosures that seal off heat exchangers, radiators, oil coolers, and so on, while forcing cool air to flow through each. Brake ducts direct cool air through hoses to cool rotors under racing conditions. Greater numbers of openings in the front of the air dam, grilles, etc., decrease the amount of downforce produced and increase drag. Teams not only control critical water-temperature and oil-temperature levels, but can tailor handling by the addition or subtraction of tape on noses.

DYNO Short form for dynamometer, a machine used to measure an engine's horsepower and test and monitor its overall performance.

Economy run Driving slower to conserve fuel.

EIRI "Except in rare instances" A term describing NASCAR's ability to enforce its decisions when there may not be a specific rule or regulation to cover such a decision.

Engine displacement The volume within an engine's cylinders, expressed in cubic inches, that is swept by each piston as it makes one stroke downward, from top dead center (TDC) to bottom dead center (BDC). NASCAR rules only allow small block V8 engines with a minimum of 350 cubic-inch displacement (CID) and a maximum of 358 CID.

Equalize Cars in superspeedway races are required to run tires with both inner tubes and inner liners, which are actually small tires inside the standard tires. When the inner liner loses air pressure and that pressure becomes the same as that within the outer tire, the tire is said to have equalized and a vibration is created.

Factory A term designating the "Big Three" auto manufacturers, General Motors, Ford and Chrysler. The "factory days" refer to periods in the 1950s and '60s when the manufacturers actively and openly provided sponsorship money and technical support to some race teams.

FIA Fédération Internationale de l'Automobile, the governing body for most auto racing around the world.

Flagman The person standing on the tower above the start/finish line who controls the race with a series of flags.

Footprint The amount in square inches that each tire touches the earth. Larger footprints enhance tire grip to track. Four equal footprints with equally applied forces would promote great tire wear and vehicle handling.

Fresh rubber A new set of tires acquired during a pit stop.

Front clip The front-most part of the race car, starting with the firewall.

Front stretch The straight on a circle track between turns four and one. Also called "front straight" or "front chute," the start/finish line is usually there.

Gear ratio The number of teeth on a ring-gear divided into the number of teeth on a pinion-gear. Different size tracks use different gear ratios to obtain optimum performance for speed and fuel economy.

Get under Outbrake an opponent on the inside of a turn and make a pass.

Greasy See Slick.

Grenaded Destroyed an engine under racing conditions, usually in a dramatic show of smoke and fluids.

Groove The best route around a racetrack; also, the most efficient or quickest way around the track for a particular driver. The high groove takes a car closer to the outside wall for most of a lap. The low groove takes a car closer to the apron than the outside wall. Road racers use the term "line."

Handling A car's performance while racing, qualifying or practicing. How a car handles is determined by its tires, suspension geometry, aerodynamics and other factors.

Happy hour The final practice of a race weekend, usually late Saturday afternoon.

Headsock A fire-resistant head mask or balaclava.

Hole shot A drag racing term for beating an opponent off the starting line and winning a race despite having a slower elapsed time. Other racers use this term to describe a good start or restart.

Hooked up Term used to describe a car that is performing excellently because all parts are working well together.

Horsepower The estimated power needed to lift 33,000 pounds by one foot per minute — roughly equated with a horse's strength.

Independent A driver or team owner who does not have financial backing from a major sponsor and must make do with second-hand equipment such as parts and tires. The term, like the breed, is becoming rarer every year.

Infield The enclosed portion of a track, which includes team garages on most oval tracks. During race weekends, this area is usually filled with large transporters, merchandise trailers, and driver and fan motor homes.

Inner liner The tire within the tire. The tires used in some NASCAR racing have a second tire inside the main tire, which meets the race surface.

Inside groove or line On an oval track, this is the innermost racing line, which is usually separated from the infield by a distinctly flat surface called an apron. On road courses, the inside groove refers to the line closest to the curbs or walls forming the inner portion of turns.

IRL Indy Racing League

Lap One time around a track. Also used as a verb when a driver passes a car and is a full lap ahead of (has "lapped") that opponent. A driver laps the field by overtaking every other car in the race.

Lapped traffic Cars that have dropped one or more laps behind the race leader after being passed by the lead driver and others on the lead lap.

Lift To raise or lift your foot off the gas pedal. Commonly used when drivers have to lift after an unsuccessful pass attempt to slow down and get back into the racing line.

Line See Groove.

Long pedal Commonly refers to a car's gas pedal because of the design. Also used to describe a brake pedal when brakes wear out because the driver has to push the pedal harder and further to slow down.

Loose A car that has more grip in the front than the rear end and tends to fishtail; a handling condition describing the tendency of a car's rear wheels to break away from the pavement, swinging its rear end toward the outside wall. Drivers often report whether the car is loose or tight so the crew can make adjustments.

Loose stuff Debris such as sand, pebbles or small pieces of rubber that tend to collect on a track's apron or near the outside wall.

Low drag set-up Adjusting a car's aerodynamic features to minimize drag, which also reduces downforce. This set-up achieves better performance on straight-aways and reduced cornering ability. "Drag" is the amount of horsepower it takes to push the car through the air. At restrictor-plate races like Daytona and Talladega, you trade drag for downforce, so you have lower drag in order to have more downforce.

Marbles Rocks and debris that collect off the racing line. If a driver enters the marbles at an excessive speed, his car will lose grip and drive perilously into awaiting hazards. See Loose stuff.

Motor mounts Supports for the engine and transmission on a race car's frame, on which the motor sits in relation to the body of the car. NASCAR requires all motor mounts to be reinforced steel or aluminum, and adjustable mounts are not allowed. NASCAR teams strive to lower the motor mounts so that the car will have a lower center of gravity and handle better.

NASCAR Acronym for the National Association for Stock Car Auto Racing. Organization founded in December 1947 by William (Bill) France Sr. and others, which sanctions races, sets rules and awards points toward championships for several types of stock cars: Nextel Cup, Craftsman Truck and Busch Grand National Series, among others.

Neutral A term for how a driver's car is handling; when a car is neither loose nor pushing (tight).

On the throttle A driver has the pedal to the metal.

Open-wheel Formula One and Indy-style race cars that are designed to have the suspension, wheels and tires exposed with no provision for fenders.

Outbrake A driver gains time and position on an opponent by applying the brakes later and deeper into a corner.

Outside groove The outside racing line. Sometimes a car will handle and perform better on the outside/inside line and a driver opts not to use the optimum groove.

Oval An oval-shaped track. Most NASCAR races are held on a track of this shape.

Oversteer When the front of a car has more grip than the rear. This is the same as a car being loose.

Parade lap The warm-up lap before a race. Drivers use this lap to warm up their engines and often zigzag to warm up tires.

Parking lot After a big crash that takes out a lot of cars, the track looks like a parking lot.

Penalty box Derived from ice hockey. NASCAR's way of penalizing drivers for infractions by holding them in the pits or behind the wall for a specified time during a race after a driver is caught doing something against the rules.

Pit stop An integral part of most racing series where drivers stop in pit row so their crews can change tires, refuel and make repairs or other adjustments.

Points race The overall competition to win the Drivers' or Manufacturers' championship at the end of the season.

Pole position The driver qualifying fastest is awarded the first starting position. This means the driver will start on the inside (relative to the first turn) of the first row.

Post-entry A team or driver who submits an entry blank for a race after the deadline for submission has passed. A post-entry receives no Nextel Cup points in NASCAR racing.

Provisional starting spot Special performance-based exemptions for drivers who do not initially qualify for a race. A position NASCAR holds open for certain drivers, such as past champions, who had trouble qualifying for the race. A driver awarded a provisional spot must start at the back of the starting grid.

Push The rear end of a car has more grip than the front. This condition makes a car harder to turn into a corner. Commonly known as "understeer."

Pushing Handling characteristics of a car where its front end tends to push or plow toward the outside wall in a corner.

Qualify During designated sessions, teams must meet established lap times to qualify for (or enter) a race based on a predetermined number of spots available.

Race rubber Race tires as opposed to qualifying tires.

Racer's tape Heavy-duty duct tape used to temporarily repair hanging body parts that might hinder aerodynamic features and decrease performance.

Rear roll center Located simply at the center of the track bar from the ground and center from the right to left mounting points. Roll centers are measured from the ground, but are relative to center of gravity. Higher roll centers exert less mechanical advantage, so lower spring rates can control roll or weight transfer.

Rear spoiler Two nonadjustable aluminum pieces attached side by side to equal a rail on the trunk of the car. Spoilers create downforce to improve the car's handling. NASCAR alters the size and angle now and then to create parity among manufacturers.

Reasonable suspicion, substance Both refer to NASCAR's drug-testing policy. Under the policy, if a NASCAR official is reasonably suspicious that a driver, crew member or another official is abusing drugs, the individual may be required to undergo testing. Substances include cocaine, heroin, PCP and other illegal drugs, as well as alcohol and prescription drugs while participating in an event.

Restrictor plate An aluminum plate with four holes in it that is placed under the carburetor to restrict air and fuel. That restriction keeps the cars from reaching speeds that NASCAR considers dangerous.

Right combination Catch-all phrase to describe why a car, team or driver has performed well or won a race. Included are engine horsepower; tire wear; correct weight distribution; and performance of the driver on the track or the crew on pit stops.

Road course A racetrack with multiple left- and right-hand turns. Generally refers to permanent, purpose-built racing facilities. Can also refer to temporary street courses built on big city streets, which were popularized in the 1980s. NASCAR's Nextel Cup series includes two road-racing venues.

Roll bars Large, sturdy bars designed to protect a driver if the car rolls over. Very functional in race cars but used more for style in production cars.

Roof flap A device made to keep the car from turning over. It works like an airplane flap and comes up when the car slides sideways or backward, to help slow down the car and keep it on the ground.

Running anywhere A car is handling so well, a driver can use any racing line (or drive anywhere). Sometimes, handling problems lead to a preferred line where the car handles better.

Running light A car is running with little fuel. Teams qualify with a light load to achieve maximum speed.

Sandbagging Allegedly failing to drive a car to its full potential in practice or qualifying, thus being able to provide a surprise for competitors during a race.

Saving the car/tires Driving a car somewhat moderately to conserve the car's mechanical parts and reduce tire wear. This allows a driver to be more aggressive during the all-important final laps.

Scrub The amount of force exerted on the tire footprint due to the different location of tire center or pivot and the actual pivot of the spindle.

Scrubbed tires The best kind of racing tires because they've had a few laps of wear to normalize the surface.

Scuff A tire that has been used at least once and is saved for further racing. A lap or two is enough to scuff it in.

Set-up The combination of settings for a car's engine, aerodynamic features and tires/wheels. Teams make continual adjustments to a car's set-up during pit stops based on driver input.

Shoot out Two or more drivers race to the end for victory.

Short track A speedway under a mile in distance.

Silly season Slang for the period that begins during the latter part of the season, when some teams announce driver, crew and/or sponsor changes.

Slick A track condition where, for a number of reasons, a car's tires do not properly adhere to the surface or get a good bite. A slick racetrack is not necessarily wet or slippery because of oil, water and so on.

Slingshot A maneuver in which a car following the leader in a draft suddenly steers around it, breaking the vacuum; this provides an extra burst of speed that allows the second car to take the lead. See Drafting.

Slip stream The cavity of low-pressure area created by a moving object. In racing, drivers use this slip stream to draft another vehicle.

Spoiler A metal strip that helps control airflow, downforce and drag. The front spoiler or air dam is underneath the car's front end near the axle; the rear spoiler is attached to the trunk lid. "Adding more spoiler" refers to increasing the rear spoiler's angle in relation to the rear window and generally aids a car's cornering ability. Less spoiler, decreasing its angle, aids straight-away speed.

Sponsor An individual or business establishment that financially supports a race driver, team, race or series of races in return for advertising and marketing benefits.

Stagger On ovals, teams may use a different size tire ("stagger") on the outside wheel to improve the car's handling ability. Also, the difference in size between the tires on the left and right sides of a car. Because of a tire's make-up, slight variations in circumference result. If the left-side tire is 87 inches, and the right-side tire is 88 inches, you have one inch of stagger.

Sticker(s) A new tire or tires. Term comes from the manufacturer's stick-on label denoting the type of tire, price and so on. Teams generally use sticker tires during qualifying, then use scrubbed tires in a race.

Stop-and-go penalty A penalty that requires a driver to stop at his team's pit for a timed penalty before reentering the race. This penalty can be assessed for anything from speeding in the pits to contact with an opponent.

Superspeedway A racetrack of a mile or more in distance. Road courses are included. Note: Racers refer to three types of oval tracks. Short tracks are under a mile; intermediate tracks are at least a mile, but under two miles; and speedways are two miles and longer.

Taped off Usually refers to applying racer's tape to the brake duct opening in full-bodied cars.

Tech Short for tech inspection, or technical inspection. Each car is submitted to tech inspection so sanctioning-body officials can confirm that all chassis and engine parts meet Series' guidelines. A "teched" car has passed inspections.

Telemetry Highly sophisticated electronics that transmit performance data from a car on the track back to team members.

Template A piece of aluminum that is placed on the cars to regulate the body sizes and diameters to make sure the body stays the way the manufacturer submitted it.

Tight Also known as "understeer." The car's front tires don't turn well through the turns because of traction loss. A driver must slow down entering and going through the turns to avoid having the car push all the way into the wall.

Tow-in The amount of distance the front tires are angled in toward the center of the car.

Track bar Connects the rear housing to the frame of the car and keeps it centered under the vehicle. It can be adjusted up and down to change the car's handling characteristics during pit stops.

Tri-oval The configuration of a racetrack that has a hump or fifth turn in addition to the standard four corners. Not to be confused with a triangle-shaped speedway, which has only three distinct corners.

Tuck under Drive closely enough behind an opponent's car to move into (or "tuck under") its draft.

Turbulence Rough air encountered by race car drivers.

200-mph tape Racer's tape, or duct tape, so strong it will hold a banged-up race car together long enough to finish a race.

Understeer When a car has more traction (or grip) in the rear than in the front.

Unlap A driver down one lap passes the leader to regain position on the lead lap.

USAC United States Auto Club

Valance The panel that extends below the vehicle's front bumper. The relation of the bottom of the valance, or its ground clearance, affects the amount of front downforce the vehicle creates. Lowering the valance creates more front downforce. Also referred to as "front air dam."

War wagon Slang for the large metal cabinet on wheels that holds equipment in the driver's pit box during the race. Also called "pit wagon."

Warm-up lap The lap before a race starts. Drivers use this parade lap to warm up their engines and tires.

Weaving Zigzagging across the track to warm up and clean off tires, or to confuse an opponent while attempting a pass.

Wedge The cross-weight difference; that is, the amount of weight on the left rear and right front of the car.

Wind tunnel A structure used by race teams to determine the aerodynamic efficiency of their vehicles, consisting of a platform on which the vehicle is fixed and a giant fan used to create wind currents. Telemetry devices determine the airflow over the vehicle and its coefficient of drag and downforce.

WoO World of Outlaws

Wrench Slang for racing mechanic.

Zigzag To move sharply back and forth on the track. Drivers often zigzag on warm-up laps to heat up their tires.

ACKNOWLEDGMENTS

I would like to thank Dave Franks, a veteran photographer who has covered the NASCAR circuit for decades. Franks has the ability to provide images that not only capture the essence of racing but the people behind the racing. I would also like to thank Steve Milton, who got me into this venture, as well as the team at Firefly, including Michael Worek, Barbara Campbell and Steve Cameron, for their support, ideas, and patience. And a big tip of the hat goes to Gareth Lind who has vibrantly brought this sport to life on these pages.

— Timothy Miller

To Smitty, for the irreplaceable gift of lifelong friendship. To my mom for the love of language, to Jess and Tobes for the love of life, and to Michelle for the power of love. To all the folks at Firefly for their consummate professionalism. And to Tim Miller for keeping me in the right gear. Thanks.

— Steve Milton

A lot happens in the garage with last minute tinkering. Here teams are getting their cars just right during practice for the Sharpie 500 at Bristol Motor Speedway, August 24, 2007.

DRIVER PROFILE INDEX